FAITH OVER FEAR
Amidst Financial Crisis

Rachel Marie

Anchored in Hope Publishing

Ms Rachel Marie / Anchored in Hope Publishing
11923 NE Sumner St
Suite 884363
Portland, OR 97250
www.msrachelmarie.com

Book Layout © 2017 BookDesignTemplates.com
Cover photo by Amanda Cantrell

Faith Over Fear / Ms Rachel Marie. -- 1st ed.
ISBN 978-1-7346146-2-6

This book is dedicated to my father without whom
I would not be the woman that I am today.

My father gave me the greatest gift anyone could give another person,
he believed in me.

— JIM VALVANO

CONTENTS

Introduction

*The person who doesn't know where his next dollar is coming from
usually doesn't know where his last dollar went.*
– Unknown

Money. It's a subject no one likes to talk about. It makes us
all uncomfortable. There's never enough of it. Dave Ramsey
has said that it's also the number one issue that couples fight
about. (Ramsey, 2018) Why? I'm not a financial expert, but
my guess would be that we all have vastly different experiences with money, causing us to all have a different
relationship with it. This can cause a lot of conflict amongst
friends, spouses and family members.

I have never really thought about my relationship with money. I never thought about money in that way before. Money
was a possession. It's tangible. It's a thing. It's not something
with which you have an emotional connection. Oh, but you
do! I simply never understood that until now.

I have experienced some of the greatest struggles of my life
over the last four years and every one involves money. The
last four years have been some of the hardest of my life. They
have also been four years of tremendous growth. Growth
that has transformed my life, but it didn't come easily. There
were many tears, there were screams, there were panic attacks, there was begging, there was praying, then there was
sheer surrender.

Throughout it all, I tried very hard to focus on all the ways
God was showing up in my life. I started a gratitude journal
to track all of the God moments, which I also refer to as God
winks, that happened in my life. I knew it would be easy to

forget all the ways God had been faithful in my life when I was facing a new struggle. I wanted to have something to look back at in those moments of doubt.

Single line entries turned into paragraphs, which turned into pages of a single story filled with details of all the incredible things that God orchestrated on my behalf. Me. This completely unworthy, sometimes even ungrateful, woman who doesn't feel deserving of God's endless amounts of grace and generosity.

During this season, it was laid on my heart to start writing this book. It was as if the Holy Spirit was telling me that there are far more people in my situation than I realized. People who are facing job layoffs, struggling to find a new job, facing foreclosure, etc. People who need their faith to be greater than their fears during a financial crisis. People who need a gentle reminder that God is in the midst of our crisis. He will meet us right in the middle.

I will admit writing this book has been one of the most challenging things I have ever done. There have been months when I wrote nothing and even thought there was no reason to see it through to completion. My ego has fought me every step of the way. There have been feelings of shame and humiliation, feelings of sadness and doubt, feelings of frustration and defeat.

Have you ever seen the quote on social media that the enemy wouldn't be attacking you so hard if you didn't have something amazing inside you? It's one of those feel good quotes that we share with our friends when they are facing trials. I wonder how often we use that same quote to shut down the enemy when we feel attacked. Do we rise up and rebuke the enemy, or do we sit in surrender to the power of our thoughts?

I should be the first to admit that I've spent many days succumbing to negative thoughts that run through my mind. They seem to be nonstop some days. These thoughts lead to anxiety. The anxiety leads to doubt. The doubt causes you to start to lose faith.

I want you to find your faith again. I want you to have hope. I want you to see God at work in your life, on your behalf, on a regular basis. I want you to live from a place of abundance instead of scarcity. I want your perspective to shift in such a powerful way that your life is transformed in the same way mine was.

I feel it's probably important at this point to give a few disclaimers. First off, I didn't know when my life started falling apart that I was going to share the things that happened next with the world. I wasn't keeping notes and writing along the way. There may be some choppy parts lacking a whole lot of substance and detail. Please forgive me. A lot has happened.

Secondly, please know that I am not a biblical scholar. There are very few verses of the bible that I know by heart and can tell you the book, chapter and verse where they are located in the bible.

Finally, I've never written a book before. I certainly never expected to write one so incredibly personal and transparent. I've made mistakes. I've not always been the best Christian. I'm certainly not here to pass judgment, criticize or condemn anyone. The opinions and perspectives shared in the pages to come are a reflection of me, my experiences, my beliefs, my convictions, and my struggles. If there's something you don't agree with, that's okay. I don't expect everyone is going to agree with my views. That's the beauty of being who we are as individuals.

As we go on this journey together, I hope you'll open your heart to receive what God wants to share with you. What better way to ensure that than opening this journey in prayer.

Dear Heavenly Father,

I am so incredibly thankful for the special soul who's reading this book right now. I believe with all my heart that you asked me to write this for a reason. Even if that reason was for it to reach just one person, this person, right now, then it was worth everything I went through to get to this point today. I ask that you give me the words to help communicate the message that you want this beautiful soul to hear. I pray that they read these pages with their hearts wide open to receive from you. Use me as a vessel to share the message of your goodness and grace. Help me to share boldly knowing that it is through my weakness that you are my strength and to whom all glory is given. May this reach those for whom it was intended.

In Jesus' name I pray,

Amen.

Chapter One

When we are children we seldom think of the future. This innocence leaves us free to enjoy ourselves as few adults can. The day we fret about the future is the day we leave our childhood behind.
— Patrick Rothfuss

Before I jump into what will likely feel like reading my diary entries, I wanted to give you some background on my life. I'll be kind and give you the CliffsNotes version. I think it's important for you to understand where I come from, what my upbringing was like, as well as the events that led up to this season of financial crisis to be able to understand the significance of each experience.

Perhaps, like me, no one ever really talked to you about money. Let alone talked about how each of us has a relationship with money - a lens through which we see it and how we feel about it. Looking back on my childhood, I can think of quite a few different memories that involve money that have a negative emotional response tied to it.

It would seem this has always been an area in my life that caused me anxiety, even from a very young age. An area with which I have always struggled to fully trust God.

Let's just jump right in, shall we?

The Early Days

For in every adult there dwells the child that was, and in every child there lies the adult that will be.
— John Connolly

I had a really good childhood, all things considered. We lived a block from the beach and I had no idea that we ever struggled with money. My mom was a waitress and my dad worked at a behavioral center for troubled kids. My mom worked during the day and my dad at night. I assume it allowed them to alternate who was home with my brother and me so they wouldn't have to pay for childcare.

You're probably wondering how a couple working such average jobs could afford to buy a house a block from the beach. Even in 1979, I'm guessing it would have been a lot less to live further inland.

You see, my dad grew up in New Jersey on a farm. He was an only child. My mom, on the other hand, grew up in the Bronx of New York. She was one of 15 children. They lived in an apartment where the dresser drawers were used as cribs. Both of my parents came from very humble beginnings.

When my parents met, they were both living in Fort Lauderdale, Florida. They decided to move north to start their family. My dad wanted to live beachside. My mom said they couldn't afford it. My dad said they couldn't afford not to. He wanted to give his children a better life. Neither of my parents wanted my brother and me to go through what they went through growing up.

I know they made a lot of sacrifices for us. The depth of which I'll never truly comprehend.

I only have one real memory of my parents fighting. If it happened any other time, it was always done away from my brother and me. But this one time, I could tell something wasn't right, so I went to my parents' bedroom door to listen. That's how I knew they were fighting, and what they were fighting about.

The mortgage was due and they couldn't pay it. $780. My mom was scared. My dad stressed. He was trying his best to provide for his family. I felt that anxiety. I took it on myself. I was scared for my mom. Sad for my dad. I knew nothing about money. All I knew to do to help was not to ask for anything.

My mom had a very strong faith. She prayed every day. Out loud. As she was cooking, doing dishes, laundry, driving in the car. It didn't matter. She always found time to talk to God. My mom loved the beach. It was her favorite place to talk to God. She would walk along the shore and pray for hours. We went to church Sunday morning, Sunday night, Wednesday night and Saturday night. We also had bible study at our house once a week.

I can remember walking down the aisle in the grocery store when a woman from our church was walking towards us. She got this great big smile on her face. She hugged my mom and me. She said, "I was planning on giving this to you on Sunday but since you're here now" and she handed my mom an envelope saying, "God laid it on my heart to give this to you."

It was a check for $1,000. A thousand dollars.

At a young age, I saw God show up and show off for my family.

My mom's best friend when I was growing up was a doctor. If we had any issues, all we had to do was go to her office. We walked in the back door through the employee entrance, hung out in her office until she was done with a patient and then she'd check on us. We never had to pay for our visits.

Whenever we needed medications, she would get us samples so we didn't have to pay for any prescriptions.

When I got older and didn't have insurance, my dad talked to his doctor during one of his appointments to see how much it cost for someone without insurance to be seen. His doctor told him to have me make an appointment and he would see me free of charge. I went to him for years and he never charged me a penny. Again, he would give me samples whenever he could so I wouldn't have to pay for prescriptions.

I couldn't really appreciate the significance of this earlier in life. I had no idea the cost of health care, medical expenses, prescriptions, etc. I was shocked when I had to go to Urgent Care once and it was $125 just to be seen.

When you stop and think about your life. I mean really think about the details. I bet you could see God at work in your past as well.

The Later Years

Parents can only give good advice or put them on the right paths,
but the final forming of a person's character lies in their own hands.
— Anne Frank

My parents really pushed education. They wanted my brother and me to have a better life, not just a better childhood. That meant you went to school, you got an education, so you could get a good job and make a lot of money.

I was never really good at anything other than school and eating. You can laugh. There's a running joke in my life at this point that I only show up for the food. School came easy for me, even after my mom died my sophomore year of high school.

My brother was the first to graduate from college. We may be a little competitive in our family so I had to one up him by going to law school and becoming the first lawyer of the family.

We were doing it right. The American dream. Or at least trying.

Except my entire law school education was funded by student loans in excess of $200,000. Maybe that wouldn't have been as dismal as it seems if I had passed the bar exam on the first try, but I didn't. Not the first time, or the second, or even the third. If I heard one more person mention it took John F. Kennedy Jr. three tries to pass, I might inflict physical harm on another human being.

It wasn't until five years after I had graduated law school that I passed the bar. By that point, the thought of being a lawyer had been put aside. I had only taken the bar exam again in hopes that I could feel as though that part of my life had closure. By seeing it through to the end, those feelings of shame, disappointment, etc. from not passing would be gone.

I started working for one of the largest banks in the country as an entry level employee. It was a customer contact center, also commonly known as a call center. I was working the night shift, which was from one o'clock in the afternoon until ten o'clock in the evening. It was perfect as it allowed me to still help out during the day at my dad's restaurant.

I was making good money at the bank. In my first year, I managed to pay off $24,000 in credit card debt that I had accumulated throughout college and law school. I think we've all learned our lesson not to take out a store card at every store where you shop (Target, Old Navy, Kohls, Victoria Secret just to name a few of the ones that I had).

After my credit cards had been paid off, I bought a new car, but made sure to keep my payment manageable at $254 a month. My next focus was on saving to buy a house.

After I had been working at the bank for almost a year and a half, I was promoted to a supervisor position. Not even a year later, I received another promotion. This time to Assistant Vice President. At this point, I was making close to six figures a year in a town where the median income was roughly half that. I was living the life. Things were good. Really good.

The next step of adulthood was to buy my first home. I saved a little over $30,000 to use towards my down payment. I found a house that was everything I wanted, except that it was a foreclosure and needed a lot of work. My realtor suggested I pass on the house, but I couldn't. Every single thing on my checklist, it had. It was the first house that offered me everything I wanted.

I never knew $30,000 could be spent so fast. Looking at it sitting in my bank account, it sure felt like a lot of money but it didn't go very far. I depleted all of my savings and started using credit cards again to complete projects that cost far more than I had originally anticipated. I should have taken a friend more seriously when he warned me that when you try to fix one problem, you usually end up with three.

I assumed that I would be able to get my credit cards paid down again, so I wasn't stressing over it. I thought I had time, but what can I say? Life likes to keep things interesting and will throw a curve ball when you least expect it.

Two weeks to the day of the one-year anniversary of buying my home, I received notice that the entire department I worked with was being laid off. I had exactly one paycheck left to my name.

I hadn't been able to save a penny for that first year. A lot of that was my own fault, trying to make a house a home by filling it with things. The truth is, I was trying to fill a void I felt internally and it was manifesting itself through a lot of unnecessary online purchases. Have you ever done that? I even bought a second vehicle after a breakup. No idea why I thought that would somehow help heal the heartache.

My best friend, Chad, was active in church. A strong believer. He wasn't afraid to bring up God with me despite my hardened heart. He was quick to tell me that I was trying to fill a spiritual void with material things, and it was never going to work. What I needed to do was get myself back to church. The only way that void would be filled was to have a relationship with God again.

The thought alone, the thought of stepping into a church, made me feel physically nauseous. I had not stepped inside a church in 19 years. As I mentioned earlier, my mom died my sophomore year of high school. At the age of 42, she passed away from leukemia.

A lot happened with the pastor of the church that I'd grown up in when my mom was in the hospital fighting for her life that made me really question the whole institution of church. I was angry. I was bitter. I was resentful. I was hurt. Mostly, I didn't trust the people who called themselves Christians. They were hypocrites.

Despite my continued resistance, Chad kept encouraging me to just start trying new churches to see if I could find one that I liked. In an attempt to get him to leave it alone for a while, I made the statement, "Maybe if I could find a new church, one just starting out, that wasn't very big that I could grow with and have it feel more like family, I'd go." I figured that would at least leave him feeling like he had made progress with me and wouldn't bring it up again for a while.

I learned quickly that God really does have a sense of humor and will call you on your bluff. I'll share more on that in a few minutes!

When I received the news that we were being laid off, I was terrified.

Seven months prior to the layoff, I had joined a network marketing company. I actually didn't realize I joined a company. I simply went for the option that allowed me to get the most products at the cheapest cost for my dad and me. Without even trying, I started receiving a monthly paycheck. The girl who introduced me to the company showed me her last paycheck, it was almost $10,000 for one month!

I thought, if she could do it, why couldn't I?

I decided to put forth all I had to grow that business. I knew if I was going to make it work, I was going to have to do things that I wasn't comfortable with – like talking to strangers! I signed up to do a vendor event downtown in hopes it would help me spread the word about the products and eventually grow my business.

I hated downtown, almost as much as I hated talking to people. The likelihood that you'd find me downtown during the monthly street party was slim to none.

I know I'm not the only one who has shot down an isle at the grocery store just to avoid having to talk to someone you recognized. Ever pretended not to know someone? I have. Ever pretended they had you confused with someone else? I have. Ever just blatantly ignored someone calling your name? Done that too.

Yet here I was, on this particular night, downtown and positioned in such a way that if someone approached me to talk,

I'd actually have to be nice and receptive. I knew it was going to be painful!

I can still remember that first night as a vendor downtown. It was cold and I didn't want to be there. I was tired of smiling and pretending to be excited about what was going on. Suddenly this girl walked over with purpose. Most people are trying to avoid anyone "selling" stuff.

"Tell me about this!" she says with so much energy.

I started sharing about the products and my experiences. She was really engaged, asking questions, and being receptive. She took some information and walked away.

I stood there thinking to myself, "I should have gotten her contact information." Have you ever met someone and within minutes you just had this feeling like you would be great friends?

A few minutes later she came back to our booth with some hot chocolate for my friend's young son. She handed me a post card. It said Elevation. I looked at her and said "what is this about? I've never heard of it."

She proceeds to tell me that Elevation is a church that's new to the area. They're just starting out and trying to spread the word about their Christmas Eve service.

I literally turned around to see if Chad was standing there trying to punk me. It was a total BUT GOD moment.

I took the post card and put it on my kitchen counter and left it there. I couldn't bring myself to throw it away. Every day I walked past it. Looked at it. Something inside me told me that I should go. I needed to go.

We've already established that I can be pretty anti-social. Nothing inside of me wanted to go alone, so I talked to a friend about it to see if she would want to go with me. She had been thinking about going back to church, so she agreed to go. I was actually excited. Crazy, right?

The day before, my friend sends me a text that her flight had been canceled due to weather and they were hoping to be able to fly the next day. But now she wasn't sure if she'd be able to go with me. My heart dropped. Immediately I thought to myself, maybe I just shouldn't go.

Isn't that typically how the enemy works? Quick to jump in our thoughts and try to steer us away from the one place we need to be the most.

The tug on my heart to go was stronger than the anxiety I was feeling about the possibility of having to go alone. I was venting to another friend about it. Her mom, who was in from out of town, overheard and offered to go with me. What are the odds?

I made it to the Christmas Eve worship experience and my life was forever changed. At the end of every worship experience, the prayer of salvation is said amongst the entire congregation for the benefit of those coming to Christ, or coming back to Christ. When Pastor Steven Furtick asked all of those who said that prayer to come into a relationship with Christ to please stand up, I stood up.

I was at a place of desperation in my life. A place of emptiness I had never experienced before. I had reached the end of myself. I suppose it's in those moments when we seek God the most. Even those who don't believe will plead with God to intervene and then they will believe.

I started attending church every Sunday. And every Sunday I felt like the pastor was speaking directly to me as if he had been watching me. I had never heard the word of God presented in such a way that I could actually apply it to my everyday life.

I remember when I was growing up, I would try to talk to my mom about things that were going on in my life and it seemed like she always responded with some variation of "in the bible it says." I would get so annoyed thinking, "I don't live in the bible".

Over the course of the next several months, I went from being distant and reserved, even closed off, to being known among people at church as the crier. I cried every Sunday. I was so overwhelmed with emotions. I could see God working in my life in so many ways.

For the purposes of this book though, I'm going to focus on all the ways God moved on my behalf in regards to my finances. I gave you a warning earlier that this would feel like reading my diary. I wish I would have kept a more detailed account earlier on to be able to provide a more eloquent story, but I never would have imagined that God would lay it on my heart to write this book. I hope you'll stick with me through to the end. I promise, the stories get better!

Let's jump into this diary of God's faithfulness, shall we?

Chapter Two

The Christian experience, from start to finish, is a journey of faith.
— Watchman Nee

I think the best place to start this journey is when I recommitted my life to Christ at the end of 2014.

As I mentioned, Christmas Eve was the first church service I had attended in 19 years. I started attending weekly once the services started up again in January. In case you thought my social anxiety had gotten any better, it hadn't. The first service was actually being held at a couple's home. That made me even more nervous. Of course, I wasn't going to go alone.

I found another friend who was looking at new churches and said she would go with me. I was so grateful that she decided to go. I knew if I had someone go with me that first time, I'd be able to go alone thereafter. I just really dislike going somewhere new for the first time by myself. It's ridiculous, I know.

The first worship experience I attended was titled, "Don't Lose Hope". Quite fitting since I was at a place in my life where I felt so incredibly hopeless. I had been unemployed for three months and only made a total of $824 from my network marketing gig.

Pastor Steven Furtick shared how we're focused only on what we see, and that is what's bringing us down. We have to believe, even against all facts, failures, and feelings.

Romans 4:20 states, "He gave glory to God." (New International Version) The Hebrew word for "glory" is kabad, which translates to weight. He gave the weight to God. I had to learn to do just that, give the weight of what was holding me down to God.

"So we fix our eyes not on what is seen, but on what is unseen, since what is seen is temporary, but what is unseen is eternal." 2 Corinthians 4:18 New International Version

I was giving too much weight to the wrong things, which is why I was losing hope. My focus was on the facts – I had no real job. My focus was on the failures – I was struggling to build my network marketing business. My focus was on my feelings – I didn't know how I was going to get through this.

Here are some of the sermon titles that followed: The Key to Change is More of the Same, The Problem is the Pattern, This May Take a While, Secret of Sustainable Success. You can't tell me that God didn't meet me right where I was at, in the midst of everything. If you know anything about network marketing, every self-proclaimed expert will tell you that success comes from consistency of doing a few things repeatedly.

I began to get involved more at church. We started having weekly eGroups (our term for a weekly bible study meetup). I'm pretty much an introvert, but I knew that I needed the connection with other Christians if I was going to be able to live my life the way I truly desired.

There was so much I didn't know. I started looking for a devotional and found one written by my pastor, Steven Furtick, that fell in line with where I was in my life. It was titled, "Greater Devotional: a 40-Day Experience to Ignite God's Vision for Your Life." I wanted more from my life. I wanted to step into what God had planned for me. I wanted to fulfill my purpose. But, what was that? What did it look like?

As I started the Greater Devotional, I was immediately smacked in the face with a truth I believed but was not true according to God's word. I felt guilty for wanting more from my life. I felt guilty for wanting success, for wanting financial abundance, for wanting to have influence.

Day 1 was The Muck of Mediocrity. "We can be so much better than we've become, because God is so much greater than we're allowing Him to be through us." Pastor Steven said to ask God to ignite in you a vision of the different life He wants you to live.

I knew that I had to stop focusing on what I wanted for my life and start seeking out what God wanted for my life. I truly believe that everything happens for a reason. You're exactly where you're supposed to be at this moment in time.

I looked at my situation and accepted that this is where I'm supposed to be right now. This is what I've been "given" to work with. I had an income stream, albeit small, from my network marketing gig. I knew the potential. I knew MY potential. I also knew that I already had people on my team who I never would have met had I not become involved with this company. I was their "leader" and I could influence through example.

My purpose became to use my platform with this company to let people see the light of Jesus through me and to hopefully transform their lives the way mine had been.

In January, my income was $937. I rank advanced three times in seven months. When I hit the third rank from the top of the company, I brought home $3800. Four times the amount of income I'd made just eight months earlier.

I was excited. I was passionate. Yet, I was greedy.

Not once did I ever give God back the first 10% of what He had blessed me with.

In the bible, the story of Abraham and Sarah is such a powerful story of trust and faith. In order for Abraham's faith to be strengthened, it had to have something to push against. Nothing is made stronger without resistance. Your faith needs a fight. It needs something to fight against so strength can arise in your life.

We have a tendency of giving up hope and faith that God is not going to do what He said He would do, so we try to do it ourselves. – UMM, hello! If this isn't me.

In December of 2015, Pastor Steven started preparing the church for our year end offering. This was new to me. I remember the concept of tithing from my childhood. I didn't have a real understanding of it. It was simply what you were supposed to do but I didn't have a foundation of scripture explaining the significance. While I sat there listening to Pastor Steven talk about how God measures our contribution in the context of our capacity, I kept thinking "I would tithe when I could afford it".

I truly believed that I could not afford to tithe. I was barely making ends meet as it was.

Pastor Steven shared with us that our challenge gives God the opportunity to show off on our behalf. Faith is the substance of what is hoped for. What could have become your rock bottom becomes your stepping stones.

My faith wasn't strong enough. My trust wasn't in the source. I continued trying to control everything in my life.

I know that I am to fix my eyes, not on what is seen, but what is unseen, since what is seen is only temporary and what is unseen is eternal (2 Corinthians 4:18). We can know the word, have it memorized, but if we do not believe it fully, wholeheartedly, it will make no difference in our lives.

Chapter Three

A journey of a thousand miles begins with a single step.
— Lao Tzu

As I went into 2016, I kept pushing hard to grow my business and my paycheck was reflecting my efforts. Yet, I still didn't give the first 10% back to God. I was struggling with a scarcity mindset.

Faithfulness and fruitfulness are inseparable. John Ritenbaugh wrote that faithfulness hinges upon what we value as important combined with commitment. (Ritenbaugh, 1998)

Citing Wikepedia "Faithfulness is the concept of unfailingly remaining loyal to someone or something, and putting that loyalty into consistent practice regardless of extenuating circumstances." (Faithfulness - Wikipedia, 2019)

I certainly felt like I was living in extenuating circumstances but I wasn't yet willing to return God's faithfulness that he had continuously shown me.

During the latter part of 2016, my sister-in-law had reached out to me to see if I would be interested in making some extra money. My brother and sister-in-law have a corporate housing company. They provide short term rentals across the state of Florida. My sister-in-law had a unit in Boca Raton that she wanted to see if I could help her with. The current guest was moving out and they had someone new moving in the next day. She needed to make sure that the unit was setup correctly and ready for the next guest. It was roughly a two-hour drive for me.

I wasn't exactly sure what all had to be done. I'll be honest. I get anxious doing something for the first time. I really dislike messing up or failing people, especially when my brother is involved. She said she would pay me and I wasn't in a position to say no. Money was tight. Tighter than it had been in a while so I told her I would do it. She sent me the stuff I needed for the new guest and I drove down to set up the apartment.

One thing I really don't like about South Florida is how hard it is to find parking. I didn't have a pass to park in the garage for the community so I had to find street parking. Parallel street parking. Jesus, take the wheel, because this girl is not a good judge of distances! But, I digress. I managed to figure everything out, got everything that was needed for the new tenant, and sent my sister-in-law everything she needed. As I was driving home, I got a notification that I received a $150 from my sister-in-law on PayPal.

I was shocked. We hadn't agreed upon an amount up front. The next week she needed me to turn the unit again. Over the course of the next couple months, I made six more trips to prepare the unit for a new tenant. The additional income was a huge blessing.

Although I desperately wanted my network marketing business to grow, it seemed to be doing quite the opposite. It was beyond frustrating. I wanted success. I wanted to show all of those people who said it was a scam that they were wrong. God had other plans.

There's no doubt in my mind that this season of my life was intended for God to help me grow in ways that I never would have grown otherwise. My life changed in more ways that September when Elevation Church hosted Code Orange Revival.

Every night was profound, but for the purposes of this book I'm going to focus on one particular sermon. On the sixth night of Code Orange Revival, Pastor Levi Lusko shared with us how giving, not keeping, leads to receiving.

Pastor Levi shared from 1 Kings 18, where Elijah had the people do the thing you would least expect when trying to start a fire. He told them to pour water over their sacrifice. You would expect that pouring water where one was going to start a fire would make such a fire impossible. It was through this act that the impossible became possible with God. God can do the impossible when he calls us to do the impractical.

Over and over in scripture, God has his people do impractical things. God is looking for faith. He's looking for us to trust Him. God will stack the deck against himself just to show how powerful He is.

As humans, we're always asking "what", when we should be focusing on the "who." It is far less about the instructions/directions given and more about who is giving them.

The water had nothing to do with Elijah and everything to do with the people. Here's why –

Water was a high commodity. They were in a three-year drought, so where did the water come from? The only real explanation was that the people from the tribes had brought it with them as their own drinking water and it was likely all they had. The people had to come together and work together in order to get the rain.

They would not have received the rain had the people tried to hang onto the only water they had.

When you keep what you have, that is ALL you have. But when you pour out, only then can God multiply it. You have to bring what's in your hands and put it in God's hands.

Proverbs 11:24 says, "One person gives freely, yet gains even more; another withholds unduly, but comes to poverty." (New International Version)

In my notes, with a big star next to it, I wrote "you've already proven that you can't do it without God. You can't pay your bills as it is."

It's giving, not keeping, that leads to receiving. They wanted water, they gave water.

Don't pray for what you won't pay for.

Don't pray for God to use you and then complain when you get used.

You will never get all that God has for you until God has ALL of YOU.

When the rain comes, you will hear it before you see it.

"I hear the sound of a heavy rain." (1 Kings 18:41, New International Version)

In our society, we say it looks like rain, but in the Bible, when God does something powerful, we always hear it before we see it. God wants us to walk by faith and not by sight. When he says he hears the sound of rain, it's because God said it would happen.

Don't get impatient. Get into prayer so you can hear God's blessings. (*To hear the full recording of Levi Lusko's sermon, visit https://www.youtube.com/watch?v=pXo-JzE1WYo).

A powerful word, right? I felt so convicted that I had tithed less than a handful of times since I had given my life to Christ almost two years earlier. During the month of September, I made $3400. A decent amount of money from a network marketing gig. But still, I didn't think I had enough to give.

For the past year, I didn't have a car payment, which was a huge blessing but my car was deteriorating quickly. In August, the month prior to Code Orange Revival, my mechanic told me that the transmission was shot and would cost several thousand dollars to fix. He recommended I trade the car in and get a new one instead as there would likely be other issues in the near future.

During Code Orange Revival, a friend from church was gracious enough to go with me to a car dealership and negotiate a deal for a brand-new car – my very first brand new car – with a three-year warranty. I was extremely thankful. The dealership gave me $4,200 for my trade-in and the finance manager reduced my interest rate to 3.94% to get the payment to be what I needed it to be.

God – won't he do it? It was the best-case scenario I could have imagined. A brand-new car for $287 a month. My trade in wasn't worth $1,000. God had been good to me, yet I was still resisting letting go of any of my income. The added monthly payment made me feel even less able to give back each month.

What happened in the months to follow sent me further into the mindset that I had to hold on tight to everything I had. I was so focused on the income I was receiving from my network marketing gig that I failed to see all the other ways God was blessing me in mighty ways.

In the month of October, my network marketing commission dropped from $3400 to $2800. My check may have been less, but my God is big.

One afternoon in October, my dad and I were working around my house and I shared with him some of the struggles I was facing in my business. Each month the checks were less and less. He wished that he was in a position to help, which hurt my heart. I should be the one helping him. My entire life he's been taking care of me, making sure all of my needs were met, that I never went without. Yet, I was also extremely grateful to have a dad who was supportive and understanding.

A few days later he called to tell me that he had just gotten off the phone with my brother. They were talking about the life insurance policies that my dad had taken out when we were little, since he sold insurance for a living at the time. My brother was cashing his out. It was worth $5,000. It might be worth looking into so I could get a little relief and get caught up on my bills.

I found a statement that I had received earlier in the year and called the number for customer service. They walked me through everything I had to do to cash in the policy. It would take 10-12 business days but the funds would be direct deposited into my account. The timing could not have been more perfect.

I was leaving in a week to go to Dallas, Texas for a conference I had earned through my company. Only the top 2% of the company attended based on sales and business growth for the months leading up to the event. We were allowed to bring a guest, so I asked my best friend Crystal to come. We had not seen each other in 10 years. The company paid for the hotel room, but I had to cover my flight and food expenses.

A deposit for $5387 was in my account the morning of my trip. It was so nice to be able to go and not have to look for the cheapest meal on the menu, or worry about how I was going to pay my part of the Uber fees to and from the airport. It was probably one of my most favorite trips. Those with whom you surround yourself truly make all the difference in the world.

I was able to get caught up on my mortgage and pay past due balances on my credit cards. It was a huge relief but the money was gone almost as soon as it was received.

Then in the month of November, my network marketing commission check dropped to $2650.

When I was working in corporate America, I originally worked for a very large company with locations all over the world. They announced that they would be laying off tens of thousands of employees within the coming one to two years. We knew that there was a chance that our site could be impacted, but we had sustained through previous mergers and acquisitions. Given how inexpensive our site was in comparison to others and the quality of work produced, we were hopeful.

I had developed an "everything will work out for the best" attitude now that I could reflect on some of my own experiences. I hope you'll indulge me while I share a little back story with you.

When I was in undergraduate school at the University of Florida, I planned on attending their law school. I had a plan. You know what they say about God when you tell him your plans? He laughs. I can testify to this. I had the GPA and the LSAT score to be accepted, but it didn't happen. They encouraged me to reapply for the Spring admissions, as I had a greater chance of being accepted. At the time, this was one of the only schools who had Spring admissions for their law school. I decided to defer my acceptance to the University of Miami for one year to give myself the chance to go to the school I really wanted to attend. But again, my application was denied.

I was so upset. I couldn't even imagine moving to Miami. My brother went to undergrad there and I had gone down to visit a few times. It was a big city for this little beach town girl, full of pretty people, skinny people, and people with lots of money. I was none of those things. I wore men's oversized t-shirts and men's jeans with sneakers every day of my life. My dad worked as a custodian at a middle school. We were blessed, but not trust fund baby blessed.

It was, for all intents and purposes, my worst dream come true. I had to take out student loans to cover tuition and living expenses. My first apartment was a 450 square foot studio that was $900 a month. Everything was so expensive. Mind you, this was back in 2003. When I went to college in Gainesville, I lived in a one-bedroom townhouse and paid $650 a month. It was double the size and had its own washer and dryer hookups, back yard, court yard, etc.

I remember going to orientation with my brother's friend. I was terrified. I kept looking at all these people who were dressed so nicely and here I was in my usual, oversized t-shirt, jeans and sneakers. I didn't own anything else. There was one girl I kept looking at. She was perfect. Perfect hair. Perfect skin. Perfect body. Gorgeous eyes. She was wearing a white button-down shirt, tucked into fitted jeans with black high heels. Simple, yet classy. I remember thinking, if I could just look like that.

The next week, classes started. The entire first year class was split up into four sections. Whoever was in your section, you would share all the same classes. I remember sitting in my very first class and she walked in! The perfect girl. She looked just as put together on the first day as she did at orientation. I looked exactly the same in an oversized t-shirt, jeans and sneakers. I don't know why, but she sat one seat away from me. Little did I know that perfect girl would become my closest friend for the next three plus years.

We were sitting in the "quad" for lunch that first week and another girl asked to join us. Through conversation, I learned that she knew my brother from undergrad. I always worry when people tell me that they know my brother. Part of me thinks the only reason they're being nice to me from that point forward is because of him. Silly? Maybe, but I could write a whole book on the issues that come from being the fat kid sibling to the star athlete. When she told me that she didn't like my brother, it made me laugh. I liked her even more now. She was also perfect. Tall. Thin. Naturally beautiful in a way that not many girls can pull off. Gorgeous long hair.

The three of us were practically inseparable from that day forward. My greatest fear was that I wouldn't have any friends, and within days of classes starting, I was never alone and always felt wanted and included. God knew exactly what I needed and provided it right on time.

My first summer, I decided to do study abroad with two other girls from school. We went to London, Paris, all over Greece, all over Italy, and to Barcelona. It was the most lifechanging experience.

My final semester of law school, I started a diet with a friend and her mom. I never expected it to actually stick, but I had lost 35 pounds before graduation. Seeing the surprised look on my dad's face when he showed up was the greatest feeling ever. I went on to lose 80 pounds that year.

What started out as the worst possible thing that could happen to me turned out to be the greatest thing that ever happened to me. I left Miami a drastically different person than when I arrived. Aside from the student loan debt, there wasn't one negative thing I took away from my time there. I often look back on this experience and remind myself that God is going to put me exactly where I am supposed to be and it's going to turn out better than I could ask or imagine.

That's what Ephesians 3:20-21 tells us about who God is, right? "Now to him who is able to do immeasurably more than all we ask or imagine, according to his power that is at work within us, to him be glory in the church and in Christ Jesus throughout all generations, for ever and ever! Amen." (New International Version)

It's easy to lose sight of all the ways that God has worked on your behalf in the past when you're so focused on the struggles you're facing in your current season.

Returning now to my time in corporate America. Everyone had been a little on edge with all the rumors about layoffs and downsizing. Even before I had come to invite Jesus back into my life on a much more personal level, I still had faith and believed that everything would be okay.

One afternoon, all the supervisors and department managers were called into a big meeting for an announcement. The head of our department had flown into town to give us the news. We were not being laid off. Instead, our site had been sold to a third-party company who would take over the day to day activity, but we would still continue to work as contract employees for the company. Our paychecks would just now be signed by someone else.

While I'm sure everyone was happy that we still had jobs, there were a lot of people who were skeptical about the transition. They tried to make it seem as though nothing was going to change and everything would be rainbows and butterflies. I will admit, I did not have the same amount of experience as many in the room. I had no other experience actually. I was looking through rose colored glasses and believed that this could become a really great opportunity.

Within two years, the company that bought our site had over extended themselves, taken on too much too soon, and were in financial crisis. The previous company decided not to renew their contract, which left 200 plus employees without work to do. Unless our employer entered into a contract with another company, we would all be out of jobs.

They gave us the news with only 14 days notice. We were being laid off. We were offered two $500 payments in severance as long as we signed away our rights to sue them. I had already been warned by a lawyer that this is often done and not to agree to it because they may not pay out final wages, sick leave, time off, etc. Legally, you have to give employees a 60 day written notice of a lay off. There was already a class action law suit against the company brought on by another site that did not get proper notice. My guess is they knew the same would happen with our site and they were trying to mitigate the damages by having everyone sign the severance package. $1,000 is better than $0.

Unfortunately, many employees did not receive their final paycheck. A group had consulted with a local attorney regarding the company's failure to give proper notice of a mass lay off. The WARN Act was passed by Congress in 1988. The Act requires that employees receive 60 days advance written notice of mass layoff. If employers do not give employees proper notice, the employees can generally recover pay and benefits. Within two weeks of my attorney sending a letter of intent to sue the company, we received word that they had filed bankruptcy. That was in July of 2015. To date, we have not received a penny that was owed from the company.

I had pretty much written off all things to do with that company until I received a notice in the mail saying due to the company closing, my 401k either had to be cashed or reinvested into another 401k program. I had completely forgotten that the company had started a 401K program several months after they took over our site. I called the number on the letter to find out what it was worth.

After cashing it and paying the necessary taxes, I was left with $844.61. It wasn't enough for a mortgage payment but it was a lot more than I currently had. I was in complete disbelief. Yet again, God provided for me in a time of need. Yet again, money showed up out of nowhere. But God, won't he do it!

It didn't stop there. A month or so later, my dad came over to my house and brought me a piece of mail that he said belonged to me. It was a quarterly statement for stocks that had been purchased for me as a minor. He explained that when I was a baby, he had invested a small amount of money in this particular stock in my name.

I opened it up and looked at the information. I knew next to nothing about stocks. I went on the website to see what the current value of the stock was. I was shocked to see it was almost $15,000. I was able to sell enough stocks to get caught up on my mortgage and all of my credit card payments. Thankfully, taxes were taken out prior to payment so I didn't have to worry about that side of it either.

It was such a relief to be caught up on everything. When commissions posted for December, my pay had dropped down to $2400. Not the direction I was hoping my check would go. December brought with it another disappointment.

Growing up, we always had a dog for as far back as I can remember. When my brother was in junior high, he wanted a rottweiler. Everyone knows the stigma associated with the breed. My parents told my brother that he had to read up on the breed, how to train them, how to socialize them, etc. to make sure that he knew what he was getting himself into. That may be the only book my brother has ever actually read cover to cover.

One day my dad came home with the most beautiful rottweiler puppy. I was forever hooked! Our first rottweiler, Azar, was always really my brother's dog. After I bought my house and felt settled, I decided to start looking at puppies. I found some online that were an hour and a half away, so I asked my friend if she wanted to ride with me to look at them.

Initially, I was set on getting the first born, the biggest, but I had all these people's voices in my head saying, you take the dog that keeps coming back to you. This one, he kept coming and getting in my lap. I'd get up to play with some of the others and he'd come back to me. I decided, that was the one for me. I originally named him Diesel because I wanted a "tough" name for a "tough" dog, except my dog was a total mama's boy. Sweet as could be. I decided to rename him Bentley because I paid a whole lot of cash money for him. My friend told me that was a lame joke, but I still find it really amusing.

When I was speaking with the breeders, I asked if there were any known hip issues with the parents. One thing I remembered from my brother's reading up on the breed was to make sure there was no history of hip issues with the father or mother's blood line. I was assured there wasn't, that he would come with AKC registration papers. I guess the excitement got the best of me and I didn't do my due diligence. I assumed, if the dog was coming with papers, he must come from a good bloodline.

Before Bentley turned three years old, he had to have TPLO surgery done on his hind leg. The local vet told me that I had two options. I could go to a clinic about an hour away, or I could go to the University of Florida Small Animal Hospital, which would be two to three thousand dollars more. I was cautioned that the less expensive clinic had done this procedure on other dogs, but they had ended up with infections. Some even died. I already had confidence in the University of Florida as I attended undergrad there and knew the quality of the work done at their hospitals. Bentley is like a child to me.

I couldn't risk him dying from an infection, so I made an appointment at UF.

We drove three hours for the consultation. I was very impressed with the veterinary student assigned to Bentley's case. She was extremely thorough explaining what they expected to find and why this happens. She told me that it was very rare for this to happen to a dog at such a young age, and the only reason it would likely happen was if there were similar issues with both the mother and the father. That was the first gut punch. Then she told me that 85% or more of all dogs who have this surgery done will end up needing it done on their other hind leg a year or two later. I wanted to cry.

She wanted me to know what I was getting myself into before they did x-rays and a physical exam to determine if TPLO surgery was necessary. Some owners choose to manage the pain with medication instead of getting the surgery done. I was grateful she gave me the information in advance if I decided against the surgery, I wouldn't have to pay the $300 for the x-rays and exam, but I wasn't comfortable with managing the pain. It was my view that Bentley couldn't tell me how much pain he was in and I didn't want him living his whole life in pain. I wanted him to live a full life, a happy life.

They walked me through everything and explained how hard the recovery period would be. It would require a lot of work for both of us. Finally, we got to the most important part. The cost. The surgery would be $4800. I explained that I didn't have the money to do the surgery the following day, so I would have to call and schedule it once I figured out how I was going to pay for it. At that time, my credit was still good. I was still paying on everything. I got a CareCredit card with a $6,000 balance and scheduled Bentley for surgery in February of 2016, despite the many people who thought I was crazy to spend that much money on an animal.

The veterinary student who performed his surgery was amazing. She took a lot of time walking me through everything, answering all of my questions. She gave me her email address so I could ask any questions that might arise after we got back home. The recovery time was three months. We had to go back to the animal hospital once a month for a checkup. Every month the veterinary student was impressed with Bentley's progress. He did perfectly. I was so happy to have that phase finished.

I knew that there was a chance we would go through this again, but I never anticipated it would be so soon. In June of 2016, the other knee had the same issue. I tried to get a balance increase on the CareCredit card to cover the expense of the second surgery, but, due to my declining credit score from late payments, they denied my request.

I absolutely hated seeing Bentley in pain again. He would cry out in pain almost daily. It was heartbreaking. I had no idea how I was going to be able to afford to get him the surgery he so desperately needed. I felt like I had failed him. I had been one of those people who felt you shouldn't get an animal if you couldn't handle the commitment of time and care. I found myself sitting on the couch thinking about all the times I passed judgment on others who would post on social media about needing to rehome their pet because they couldn't afford the additional expenses the animal brought. Now, here I was in that exact same position.

Out of the blue in November, I got a phone call from my dad's girlfriend. Although we talk a lot in person when we see each other, we don't call each other, so I was a bit surprised to get a call from her. Once we got past the pleasantries, she told me that she wanted to give me the money so that Bentley can have his surgery. I was absolutely floored. Within days, I had a check for $4,000 and made the appointment to get Bentley his second surgery. I decided to use the $4,000 to pay off Bentley's first surgery so it was within the interest free window, and then use the CareCredit again for the second surgery. That made the most sense to me to avoid having to pay the interest.

When I made the appointment, I asked if it was possible to have the same veterinary student on his case. She had been so good with him the first time, and she knew his history. Thankfully, she was still finishing her year in the surgical portion of her education. When I brought Bentley back, he remembered her. She was tall, taller than me. Probably 5'10, and half my weight. She went to squat down to give him attention. He knocked her on her butt and proceeded to sit in her lap! We both laughed and I told her, "Sorry, he's used to dealing with a bigger girl."

As we talked through everything, she told me that Bentley had developed some arthritis in his leg, which was likely due to the delay in getting the surgery. While the surgery would help repair the tear in the ligament, there was nothing they could do for the arthritis. My heart sank a little. Again, I felt like I failed him. I explained the reason I couldn't get the surgery sooner was because I didn't have enough money on my CareCredit card and they wouldn't increase my limit.

She extended me a lot of grace in that moment and made sure that I didn't feel at fault for what Bentley was going through. She told me that she would do everything she could to reduce the cost of the surgery. One example she gave was a cooling machine they typically use every 4 hours that costs $150 each time. To reduce the total cost, she said she would have them use the machine every 8 hours instead during the 24 hour period after surgery when they keep him for observation.

When I went back to pick him up, the veterinary student came in and told me that everything went really well. She walked me through everything again, then she pulled out the bill summary. I expected it to be much of the same. She reiterated that she had cut out whatever she could that was not absolutely necessary. She flipped to the last page and put her finger on $2,800, looked at me and said, "I'm pretty sure this is wrong, but I'm not going to go through it or say anything."

I looked at her in disbelief and thanked her. That was probably the best Christmas present I could have received that year. Not only was Bentley on the road to recovery, but it cost significantly less than expected. Blessings upon blessings.

I was incredibly grateful. God had shown up for me yet again. I knew that I had to make a change. I had to start trusting God more. He had proven himself over and over again, and yet I still didn't fully trust him in the one area he was testing me the most in.

Holding onto what I had was not helping me. I was not receiving more.

I made a decision going into 2017 that I would tithe every month no matter the size of my paycheck. No matter if I didn't have enough money to pay my bills. No matter what. I was going to trust God with my finances.

Now I know, you're thinking that this story is going to transition into a series of good things happening. My business growing. My paycheck growing. I wish it was that easy.

But I will tell you this, God showed up repeatedly, just not in the ways I would have preferred.

Chapter Four

Every day I feel is a blessing from God. And I consider it a new beginning. Yeah, everything is beautiful.
— Prince

In December, I told my brother if he wanted to get me something for Christmas, I could really use a new cell phone. This was the first of many blessings to come. Not only did my brother get me a brand-new iPhone but he also put me on his cell phone plan. When I asked him how much it would be a month, he told me not to worry about it.

One less bill I had to worry about paying. My cell phone bill was roughly $100 a month.

In January, I stayed true to my commitment and tithed even though my check was $2300. God had already showed me that things would work out for my good; I just had to trust in Him.

$230 isn't a lot of money, but it was a lot of money to me. As I sat down at my laptop to tithe online, I started praying, "God, I'm scared but I'm trusting you," with tears running down my face. I didn't know how I was going to be able to pay my bills.

My faith and trust were tested in a mighty way the following month. My check was only $1700. How was I supposed to tithe when my check was $600 less? All I kept thinking to myself was *this is what I get for tithing? This is what I get for trusting?* The devil was working over time trying to convince me that my God wasn't faithful. I felt so defeated, but I put it aside. I knew I was being tested. I knew the devil was trying to kill, steal and destroy my relationship with Christ.

Again, I prayed as I submitted the payment online. Tears running down my eyes over a measly $170. That $170 seemed like so much money.

If your mailbox is anything like mine, it's mostly full of junk mail. I don't even open half of my mail. It's obvious, based on the color of the paper or the printing on the envelope, that it's a solicitation. A pre-approved credit card. A sales ad. Refinance your home with our company promotion.

I had gotten to the point where I didn't want to check my mail. It was never good news. It was either ads or bills. Looking at bill statements unsure if I'd have the money to pay them, didn't exactly make my day.

I remember worrying about how I was going to be able to buy groceries until I got paid.

I have no idea why on this particular day I decided to check my mail. It was probably because it was coming up on 14 days. If you don't empty your mailbox at least once every 14 days they'll take all your mail out of your mailbox and hold it at the post office.

I walked inside and started sorting through all the ads and solicitations. There was an envelope that wasn't clearly garbage so I opened it.

Apparently, there had been a class action law suit against the company that put on the bar study course I took after law school. I have no idea why they were sued. All I know is, because I had registered for and paid for their course during a certain time period, I was immediately included in the class action.

In the envelope was a check for $197. To say that I was elated would be an understatement. That was the biggest blessing at that time. I had no idea where I was going to get any extra money – but God, won't he do it!

That wouldn't be the last time that God would show up on my behalf when I least expected it.

January 2017

Once I purchased my new car in September of 2016, I started to let go of some of the credit cards I had. The minimum payments were more than I could afford. I tried to make sure to always pay certain ones so that I would have them available to use, such as the Care Credit for my dogs.

I was two months or more behind on almost all of my bills. I will admit that I have not always been a good steward with my money. I didn't know what else to do but ask for help. Asking for help is really hard for me. I think it's hard for most of us.

I reached out to my dad's girlfriend and asked if I could borrow $2500 so I could get caught up on some of my bills. She was kind enough to agree after we discussed what steps I was taking to change my current financial situation and the likelihood that I would be able to pay her back.

Once I received the check in the mail, I immediately made my mortgage payment as well as some other bills. I thought I would be okay if my check stayed consistent the next month.

February 2017

My commission check dropped from $2338 in January to $1756 in February. Panic started to creep in.

When I moved back home after law school in 2006, I started taking two classes a semester at the local community college to defer my student loans. I decided to take a drawing class and a pottery class. I'd never done pottery before but I loved going to places like Fire It Up where you get to glaze a piece and they fire it for you. I absolutely fell in love. Never in my life could hours of time pass where I thought about absolutely nothing but what was right in front of me.

I had taken 3 semesters of pottery and the only options left were to take it as an audit, which wouldn't work for the purposes of enrollment to not pay my loans. I started looking on websites for pottery equipment. I found a woman who lived 3 hours away that was selling her entire studio for $1500. My dad borrowed a friend's truck and we went to get it. She had absolutely everything you could imagine. She even made her own glazes. It was far beyond my expertise but it was such a good deal that I couldn't pass it up.

I created my own studio in my dad's garage and spent hours upon hours making pottery. I even created an Etsy shop and had success selling all my pieces despite their lack of grandeur.

Life happened and I moved out of my dad's house and pottery became less and less of a focus. It had been years since I used any of it, so when finances started to become an issue, I decided it was time to sell it all. I had bought 100 pounds of clay and tons of different glazes for which I was hoping to recoup my costs. I posted in various Facebook groups that were for pottery equipment trying to sell it for $2500. Then I dropped it down to $2000.

I had a local woman, who owns her own studio that is open to the public come over to look at the wheel and kiln. She wasn't interested in all the other stuff because she already had her own. She wanted a kiln with a timer feature, which mine didn't have. She told me that there was no way I was going to be able to sell everything together. She had a huge studio in Texas with 6 different kilns and a bunch of wheels, lots of equipment, etc. and she had to sell it all individually. I felt a little defeated. I told her that I was hoping to find another Rachel, someone who wanted to be able to have everything at home to work on when they had time. She wished me luck but said it was unlikely.

I decided to drop the price to $1500. A couple weeks went by and someone commented on it asking if it was still available – I told her it was! I looked at her profile and she was in Wisconsin. Bummer! (I'm in Florida just in case that hasn't been mentioned yet)

We start chatting and she tells me that she loves to do pottery as a hobby but that the studio is about 30 min to an hour away from where she lives and it makes it inconvenient at times to just go work on something and come home after a day of work. She wanted to have everything at home so she could just go down to her basement and work on her pieces. She said she was going to see what she could do and would be in touch.

The next day she asks if I would be available on a specific day in two weeks for her to come get everything. She had taken time off of work, found a cheap flight, and was going to rent a U-Haul to take everything back. I was like WHAT?! Is this really happening?

She text me when her flight landed, let me know that they were working to get a truck and would keep me posted on when they would be arriving. She had decided to make it a father-daughter trip because her dad didn't want her driving that far of a distance by herself.

I had everything boxed up and ready for her. When they pulled up, we started loading everything. My dad came over to help as well. It was comical watching two men in their late 60's to 70's trying to load this stuff and organize it so it was best situated so nothing would fall or break. You know how men are – always the smartest in the room. Ha! I say that with nothing but love.

She handed me an envelope with 15 one hundred-dollar bills in it. I wanted to cry. In that moment, I knew that my mortgage was getting paid. She told me that when she first decided she wanted to start looking for equipment, she had come up with $1500 as the maximum she could spend but as she was pricing kilns, some of them were $1500 alone. The ones that were significantly less didn't work and were being sold for parts. When she saw my post for an entire studio for $1500, she took it as a sign. She was able to use miles for her flight so it cost her next to nothing. The only other expense was for the rental truck, which was more than she anticipated but she said it was worth it to be able to not just get an entire studio but to spend the time with her dad as well.

In December, almost a year later, I went live on Facebook to share about God's faithfulness and I shared this as an example of the way that God had shown up when I least expected it. What a blessing she had been in my life at that time when I needed it so much. I think we often get so focused on the blessings we want to receive that we forget all the ways that we get to be used as a blessing to someone else. She had watched the video and commented "YOU are a blessing. The pottery equipment was everything I asked for and so much more. More equipment than I thought I could ever have with the little bit of money I had set aside. A $38 flight from Milwaukee to Orlando sealed the deal. A vacation adventure with my Dad which I will never forget. A soul nourishing outlet. And you. I asked for a little and received so much. Our combined stories of a little pottery studio will always warm my heart."

Let this be a reminder to you that when a (wo)man tells you something is impossible; nothing is impossible when God is involved. Not only is nothing impossible, but God will do abundantly more than we could ever ask or imagine.

April 2017

My commission for March and April were roughly $1950 each month. After paying the absolute basic bills (mortgage, car and car insurance), that left me with roughly $200. My electric and internet bill would be more than that.

In April, I got a quarterly statement from my previous employer regarding my pension. I completely forgot that we had pensions. I thought the only thing we had was the IRA that had been transferred. I logged onto their website to see what the balance was. To my surprise, it was over $4,000. I was able to cash it out and get $3840 after taxes.

Again, I worked to get caught up on my bills. The anxiety had reduced some and there was hope that everything was going to be okay.

May 2017

I woke up one morning, the last week of May, and as I stepped off the last stair my foot was almost covered in water. I looked around and there was water everywhere. My heart started racing. I wanted to cry but there was no time. I ran into the garage, where there was also water, grabbed my one-gallon ShopVac that's a handheld and ran back inside to try and start getting the water up. It took over an hour. My back was on fire and in a tremendous amount of pain.

I determined the water was coming from where the water heater was. I turned off the water to the house so it would stop flooding.

I just stood there looking at my floor, which was cheap wood laminate wondering if I could escape this without having to pull up all the flooring.

My dad told me to call the insurance company and see if damage from a water heater was covered. So, I called. As I was explaining what happened, the tears started running down my face. I was so scared. I had no money to pay for anything extra. Let alone something this extensive.

The representative with the insurance company was very kind. She explained that she was dispatching someone from the water mitigation team and they would be to the house within 30 minutes.

When the guys arrived, he jokingly said how impressed he was that I was able to get up all of the water using such a small ShopVac. I told him that's the impact of panic. All I kept thinking was, are the floors going to be able to dry out. He shook his head and said no, this is all ruined. He explained that they would be taking up all of the laminate flooring because almost every room on the first floor had water damage. They went room by room to determine how high the water had been absorbed into the drywall. They took pictures of every room with an infrared light that showed water damage. Then they started going to work.

They took off the baseboards in every room downstairs and proceeded to take up the laminate flooring. It was in the living room, dining room, laundry room, both downstairs bedrooms and the guest bathroom. They had to move all my furniture room by room to be able to get all the flooring up.

While all of that was going on, the insurance adjuster came to the house to take picture of everything and make an assessment. We went out to the garage for him to see how much water damage had been done there. When I bought the house, I had taken all of the cabinets from my kitchen and put them in the garage when I redid the kitchen to have storage space. The insurance adjuster said that the bottom cabinets were completely ruined by the water because they were made of formica and not wood. I explained it wasn't a big deal since they were from the kitchen anyway. He said because there was a whole set in the garage (we even hung the top ones on the wall) that he had to include all of them as a set. He was required by law to include it in his report so that if anything should happen again, I couldn't claim it then. I understood. Laws come about many times after learning from experience there's a need for them and I know that insurance fraud is a huge issue.

While he was chatting away, he said something that I didn't really understand or grasp the significance of at the time. He mentioned that I didn't have to replace the cabinets if I didn't want to. Instead I could allocate the funds to replace them towards my deductible. I had to ask what my deductible was because I couldn't remember. When he told me $2,500 I almost started to cry. I was on emotion overload.

In order to pull the moisture out of everything, they brought in these huge dehumidifiers that were extremely loud and put off a significant amount of heat. There were also fans running in every room. Thankfully, it hadn't sat long enough for mold to start.

The house was so hot from the equipment running continuously. I have two dogs – a rottweiler and a bulldog. I couldn't go to a hotel. Even if I didn't have the dogs, I couldn't afford it. I had both of my cats and my two dogs upstairs with me in my bedroom with a window A/C unit. It was rough. The dryers had to stay on for 5 days. The house had to be over 100 degrees.

What happened next, I was not prepared for. I received my electric bill and it was 3 times higher than previous months and my water bill, well, it was 100 times higher. I started crying. I called the electric company to see if there was any type of program for these situations. There wasn't. I called the local utility company to see if there were any programs for when pipes burst. There wasn't. But the woman on the

phone told me to talk to my insurance adjuster about it because there were some companies that would cover the cost
as part of your insurance coverage.

I sent an email to my insurance adjuster and told him what
was going on. He forwarded the email to someone in the
company and asked them to help me. The guy responded
back almost immediately and said to provide him with the
prior 3 months bills for each so they could get what my average expenditure was for water and electric. Anything above
that, they would send me a check for. I did it immediately
and that same day he had mailed out a check to cover the additional expense for each. I was so beyond thankful.

I want to make sure to mention that I did not want to call the
electric company or the utility company. My pride didn't want
me to. It's embarrassing to admit that you don't have an extra
$250-$300 to cover for a home emergency. But had I not
called, I may have never been told to ask the insurance company. I may have never received that financial blessing.

Once the fans and dehumidifiers were removed, things went
back to some semblance of normalcy. If you can call walking
on concrete floors with all your furniture in every room being
pushed to the center normal. I moved my living room furniture back so I could at least continue to watch tv, use the
internet, try to work on my business, etc.

A week and a half after the house flooded, I had a flight
booked and a hotel room reserved in Las Vegas for my network marketing company's convention. I had so much guilt
over what was going on at home that I didn't think it would
be right for me to go. But God – that's all I can say.

I had several people send me money via Facebook messenger
($20, $40, $50) to put towards my trip. A girl on my team had
already paid for her room and said I could stay with her and
not worry about the cost. She told her mom about what hap-

pened and her mom gave her $150 to give me to cover my food while I was there. I was so overwhelmed by people's generosity for something that most people would think was more of a luxury than a necessity.

When I got back from my trip, the project manager in charge of getting my house back to livable came over to discuss my options. I told him if at all possible, I would really love to have tile instead of wood laminate. He said that tile is quite a bit more due to materials and labor costs but he would see.

While we were in the garage looking at the cabinets, I told the project manager what the inspector had said about not replacing the cabinets and it be put towards the deductible. Thankfully it made perfect sense to the project manager. He started flipping through his paperwork and said they had quoted $4200 to replace the set of cabinets in the garage and my deductible was $2500 so I had a balance of $1700 that would probably give me enough to be able to do tile in the house.

But God!

Not only did I not have to pay my $2500 deductible. I got tile all throughout the first floor exactly how I wanted it. I also got 5-inch baseboards all throughout the first floor (as opposed to the older 3-inch baseboards). Let me tell you really quick about the baseboards. When I bought the house, I replaced the tile in the family room and kitchen. I saved all the baseboards knowing I didn't really have the extra funds to have them professionally redone. I painted all of them and attempted to put them back up. I say attempted because it was bad. I couldn't get them to fit the same. Some wouldn't stay nailed to the wall. It was a mess and looked terrible.

And now, after having gone through this horrible ordeal, my house looked amazing. It was how I had always wanted it but couldn't afford.

But God – won't HE do it! It's amazing how something that seemed like the "end of the world," from a financial perspective, ended up being one of the biggest blessings.

August 2017

One of my best friends, Sarah, is a nurse. She told me that in Ohio, where she lives, you can get paid for giving plasma. I had no idea what plasma even was. She explained it was similar to giving blood, but instead of just drawing the blood, they filter it and take out the plasma, then return the blood to your body. I had never given blood before. My only experience was at the doctor's office when you had to get blood work done. I decided to look into it.

Plasma is a transporting medium for cells and a variety of substances vital to the human body. It contains attack molecules called antibodies to fight infection, clotting proteins to help stop bleeding, albumin, which is an important protein that stops water from leaking out of the blood vessels and protects nutrients, hormones, and some medications. Plasma donations are used to produce therapies that treat diseases and disorders such as hemophilia, primary immunodeficiency, and a genetic lung disease. It is also used in the treatment of trauma, burns and shock.

The more I read, the more I learned of the importance of plasma, and the lack of committed donors. While it may have started out as a need for extra money, I realized that I could help children, like my friend Jeremy's son who has hemophilia. We live in such a fast-paced world that it's easy to lose sight of things that we ourselves don't have to deal with on a regular basis. No one is more guilty than I am of having an "out of sight, out of mind" mentality with many things in life.

I found a plasma center locally and decided to check it out. I was surprised by how much documentation you have to bring with you and the amount of paperwork. You have to do this

30 something question review to determine if you're eligible to give. One way to be disqualified is if you've had a new tattoo within the last year. I guess it makes sense given the concern with HIV.

If you pass the first screening, you get called back for a physical. It's not as invasive as one done at a doctor's office but they still require another female to be in the room if your nurse is a male. You get asked about what you ate that day, how much water you consume regularly, and they check your veins too and rate them on a scale of ease to access. You get a finger prick so they can test the amount of protein in your blood. Lastly, they take your blood pressure and I knew mine would likely be high because I was so nervous. I had also taken a pre-workout like supplement prior to going to the gym and thought that could affect it as well. Sure enough, my blood pressure was too high. He told me that I could come back the next day, but to make sure not to take any pre-workout.

I was disappointed. I really needed money for groceries and I was hopeful that I could make an extra $100 that week by giving plasma twice. Every center is different, but at mine, you got $40 on your first visit, $60 on your second, $40 on your third and $60 on your fourth. You could go twice in a seven-day period. After your fourth "donation," and I say it like that because it's not really donating if you're getting money for it but that's what they refer to you as, a donor, the amounts drop to $25 and $30.

I went back the next day and it was a different guy who would be doing the physical. Thankfully, I didn't have to go through everything again. He looked at my blood pressure and was like, "Whoa, that's high." I think he could tell that I was nervous and uncomfortable. He didn't give me a chance to say anything before he started trying to put me at ease. He started talking about how he understands, sometimes when people first become donors it's because they need money to buy groceries. As much as we all like to do for others, this isn't a particularly enjoyable experience and most people, while not all, but most people are there because they need the money, so he understood. I nodded in agreement.

Thankfully, I was right on the cusp of being able to donate that day. It was a painless process and lasted about an hour. I learned over time that the more water I drank the day before, the faster the process was. I had to drink a minimum of two gallons of water the day before and I tried to get a gallon in the morning of. I ended up donating 23 times during 2017 and was able to bring in an extra $790.

I can tell you without hesitation, had it not been for those 23 donations, there would have been many days that I would have gone without food because I simply did not have the money to buy any. I would not have had money for gas. It wasn't a lot of money, but it was exactly what I needed at that time. God never allowed me to go without.

September 2017

When I was working in corporate America, I worked for one of the largest financial institutions in the world. Our department worked with borrowers who were three months or more behind on their mortgage. Most, if not all, were facing foreclosure. We worked with everyone to try to modify their loan to get them into an affordable payment to be able to keep their home. Never in my life did I imagine that one day I would be on the other end of that phone, asking someone to please help me.

My mortgage is based off an income that no longer exists. Even when my network marketing business was at its best, I still wasn't making half of what I had made in corporate America. I did everything I could to make sure that my mortgage was paid every month but then life happened and one month I couldn't pay it because I had to pay other things.

I applied for a loan modification but was denied because I don't make enough money. Seems a bit ridiculous when that's the exact reason why I need the modification. I was fortunate enough to speak to a customer service representative who showed me empathy and truly seemed to want to help. He suggested that I apply for the Florida Hardest Hit Fund. He said that he saw a customer who was three months past due and the Hardest Hit Fund not only brought them current but paid the next three months mortgage payments as well.

A glimmer of hope. I found the website with the application and started the process. It was even more in-depth than applying for a modification. I printed everything out and mailed it in. I knew from working at the bank that faxing could be an expensive nightmare. You have to pay regardless of whether the recipient actually receives all the documents. I was assigned a case worker who went over all of my documents with me and let me know what else was needed.

In order to apply, I had to have filed my 2016 taxes. The extension was not sufficient. I had been putting off completing my taxes because I was already making payments for the prior year and I couldn't afford to have to pay any more. I felt stuck. I didn't know how I was going to be able to get my taxes done, pay what needed to be paid, and get the paperwork to the case worker in time to save my house.

At the time, I had been exercising every morning with my friend Alison from church. I explained to her what was going on and she said to let her husband help me with my taxes. They have been self-employed for 20 years and he's very familiar with the tax laws. I needed help and I certainly wasn't in a position to decline, so I reached out to her husband. He told me to put together a list of several deductions that he would need in order to file. They invited me over for dinner and a movie while her husband worked on my taxes. He went through everything and when he was done, I was getting a refund in the amount of $115.

I was in shock. How was that possible? He told me to print out the forms and look over what he did, and then file an amendment to my 2015 taxes as I likely did them wrong. I was so excited. Not only were my taxes done, but I didn't have to pay anything. On top of that, the $115 refund was applied towards the balance owed for 2015 leaving my final payment to be less than $35. So many victories through one small act of kindness.

I submitted the 2016 returns to the case worker and she sent my file off to underwriting for review. In usual fashion, they returned it to her wanting additional information. I had to contact the companies who serviced the pensions and IRA that I had cashed out to get a statement that there were zero funds left available. I had to provide my PayPal statement and explain every deposit and expense. If there was a deposit over $100 in my bank account, I had to explain the source and frequency. I gave them everything they needed and prayed it would be approved.

At this point, I was now two months past due on my mortgage. My anxiety was very high. I didn't know what I would do if they didn't approve it. I reached out to the case manager to see if she had any updates or knew when we could expect to hear. Unfortunately, she didn't know. I waited and waited. We were coming up on mid-month and I was going to be due for three months' worth of mortgage payments.

My phone rings and I see it's the Hardest Hit Fund office. I answer the phone and my case worker says she has good news. I have been approved. I was so happy. I asked her if that meant they would bring the loan current. She said yes. I asked if I had been approved for any additional assistance, as the bank had told me how someone had gotten their mortgage payed for an additional three months. She said, "Oh, you're approved for an entire year. We will bring the loan current, pay all late fees, and then pay your mortgage for the next 12 months."

An entire year? They were going to pay my mortgage for an entire year? No way! This was so much better than I even imagined.

Before it would be official, I had to come in and sign all the paperwork, then they would notify my mortgage company. The next available appointment was the following week. I didn't know if I should make a payment on my mortgage or wait. I did not want it going into foreclosure. I called my mortgage company to tell them I had been approved but they said until they received the official documents from the Hardest Hit Fund, nothing would change on my account. They could exercise their right to start the foreclosure process.

I didn't make a payment. I knew from my experience in underwriting that making a payment could disrupt their figures, which would require them to rework the file, causing further delays. I couldn't risk that. I had to just trust that God was in control and even if they did start the foreclosure process, it would be halted once they received the paperwork.

When I went to the office to sign all the paperwork, the case worker explained to me that they would be putting a lien on my house for the full amount that someone could possibly receive under the terms of the Hardest Hit Fund. This way, if I were to apply a second time under the other option, they would hold their lien position. It made sense but it didn't make me happy that there was now a second lien in the amount of $40,000 plus dollars on my house.

I asked if the money would be considered income for tax purposes and she wasn't sure but didn't think so. The money did not have to be repaid either. As long as I lived in my home for the next five years, the entire amount would be forgiven. I felt such a huge wave of relief, as if I could finally breath. I absolutely love my house. God gave me everything I wanted when I found this house, and I knew he wasn't going to let me lose it. Not like this.

There would be quarterly reviews to make sure that I was still in need of the assistance. If my situation improved, then there was the chance the assistance would stop so that there was more money available to help others in need. Seemed like a fair enough policy to have in place. I certainly wanted others to be able to feel the sense of relief that I had.

I made a post on Facebook about it in case there was someone I knew who was facing a similar struggle. Even though I had worked with borrowers in default, and we knew about the Hardest Hit Fund, it was a talking point for us to suggest for people who had been denied loan modifications. I never really understood exactly how it worked or how much it could help.

A woman who had attended an eGroup with me a year or so prior messaged asking for help with it. She had been injured and out of work. She was six months past due on her loan and her mortgage company was starting the foreclosure process. I went over to her house with my laptop because she didn't have a computer. We completed all of the paperwork and submitted it. A month or so later she sent me a text saying that they had been approved. She was crying tears of joy. She never would have known such a program existed if she had not seen my post.

It was in that moment that I realized the power of sharing one's story. There is no shame in the fact that you've been laid off and unable to get a job. There's no shame in donating plasma or applying for government assistance. Telling your story helps others to know they are not alone. You may also have knowledge they don't have that could help them find relief. I don't know about you, but I don't want anyone going through the financial struggles I've been facing. If I can help to alleviate such a situation in any way, I will gladly do so.

Owning your story is by far the bravest thing you will ever do.

November 2017

After I finished getting everything taken care of for the Hardest Hit Fund, I decided to do as Alison's husband had said and take a look at my 2016 taxes. I know I've talked about my independent nature at various points. It's definitely a blessing to be able to do things on your own, but it can also be a hinderance as well. My ego wants to believe that it doesn't need help from others. I am smart enough to figure things out on my own.

When I compared my 2016 and 2017 tax returns, there were a lot of things I didn't know I could deduct since I was self-employed. Using the 2017 return as my guide, I pulled all of my 2016 bank statements. I spent hours going through everything. I had a legal-size envelope full of receipts from work trips and such.

When I finished, not only did I not owe any money for 2016 but I was actually eligible for a refund. Who would have ever thought? Am I right?

It took about eight weeks for the IRS to complete their review and process the refund. I received a check for $3,922.25. I got the $2300 back that I had paid, interest that had accrued on those funds, and the refund for which I was eligible.

It was such a blessing and couldn't have come at a better time.

Chapter Five

I hope that in this year to come, you make mistakes. Because if you are making mistakes, then you are making new things, trying new things, learning, living, pushing yourself, changing yourself, changing your world. You're doing things you've never done before, and more importantly; you're doing something.
– Neil Gailman

There's always this sense of hope as we start a new year. We are full of grandiose ideas that this year is somehow magically going to be different than the one before. We're going to keep our resolutions. We're going to see amazing change. We're going to transform our lives.

One thing I know I'm guilty of is expecting to see God's blessings in my life after I've been obedient for a little while. As if my obedience in tithing consistently for a year meant I was now somehow entitled to this huge financial blessing. I hate to report that it doesn't work that way. At all.

God doesn't experience time the same way we do. A year to us is but a second to God. By far the greatest lesson you'll learn while waiting on God is patience.

March 2018

When I had gone through a breakup, while working and making good money, I convinced myself that I needed a second car - a SUV. If I was going to do craft shows with my pottery, I needed to have room to transport everything I would need to set up as well as all the pieces to sell.

I couldn't get a basic SUV, it had to have leather and navigation. At least I still had some sense about me to get a used car and not spend a lot of money on it.

I had the SUV for maybe two weeks when my dad's car started falling apart. The AC went out and some other things were going wrong. I told him he could use the SUV as long as he needed to. Well, for four years, my dad drove it. It started to have transmission problems, brake problems, power steering problems, and the electrical system for the radio didn't work.

The car, while valued at two thousand dollars, was not something I could sell to someone else with a clear conscience. It needed thousands of dollars in repairs. It probably wasn't safe to drive more than 20 miles.

My dad told me about these companies that buy junk cars. They will come to your house with a tow truck and pick it up.

I went online and found a local company, then entered the information about my car to get an offer for what they were willing to pay. It came back $505.

I won't lie. I was hoping it would be more like $1,000. But I couldn't complain about $505 that I didn't have 5 minutes prior.

Within a few days I had a check in my hand as I watched the tow truck pull away.

April 2018

In April, my brother approached me and asked me if I would be interested in working for him and my sister-in-law. As I mentioned before, my sister-in-law has her own business and needed an assistant to help her. My commission check had dropped down to $1500. If I had to pay my mortgage, I wouldn't have any money to cover any other expenses.

I was grateful for the opportunity to bring in additional income. It wasn't a lot of money as the base pay was $600 every two weeks. I would have the opportunity to earn a bonus each month based on production. It was a slow time of year, but the extra $1150 was a blessing.

July 2018

I decided to take a look at the stocks my dad had purchased for me as a child to see if there was anything left that I could sell. Instead of receiving quarterly profits, which would have been minimal at best, I had them reinvested. When there was enough money, they would buy more shares.

I logged into my account to see what the balance was. There was just enough to cover one months mortgage payment. There were also 50 shares that were on a stock certificate. The only way to sell them would be to provide the actual certificate. I looked through all my dad's important papers but I couldn't find a stock certificate.

I went ahead and sold the remaining stocks that I could sell so I could pay my bills. Even with my mortgage being covered through September, I was still struggling to meet my other obligations. I'll be honest, I don't know how people survive who have children. Life is so expensive just as a single person, let alone raising a family.

October 2018

September was the last month that the Hardest Hit Fund was covering my mortgage payment. It had been such an incredible blessing and relief knowing that no matter what, I was not going to lose my house. I was not at all prepared for what the month of October would bring.

In October, my commission check had dropped down to $1188. I made $1475 working for my sister-in-law. I was trying to pay on my student loans, which was $500 a month, as well as my credit cards I had left. It was so important for me to keep paying on my Care Credit card in case anything happened with the dogs. It would be the only way that I could cover the cost.

I had filed a tax extension for 2018, which allowed me to put off filling until mid-October. As a 1099 employee, I'm never sure if I'm going to owe taxes or not. This is always a source of anxiety for me; however, a benefit to working for my sister-in-law was the amount of tax write offs. There was a lot of traveling, and half my house was used to store equipment and supplies.

I was thrilled to discover I was getting $480 back in taxes from all that was paid in through the sale of the stocks. The excitement was quickly replaced with fear and anxiety.

The month of October brought with it two devastating blows. First, I was terminated by my network marketing company without explanation. They refused to tell me why I was terminated except that I had violated their policies somehow. Even though my monthly commission check had dropped down to $1200, it was still money that I needed to meet my monthly obligations.

Here I was. Monthly expenses increasing with my monthly income decreasing by almost the same amount. But that wasn't all.

There are some things that I don't think you're ever really prepared for. You may know that something is a possibility. You may know that it's happened to other people, but you don't think it will happen to you.

For me, it was the moment there was a knock on my door and heard those infamous words "You've been served." A process server handed me a Complaint filed by one of the companies that carried my student loans. The complaint was in the amount of $167,442.25 with $15,000 in damages.

As if that in and of itself wasn't overwhelming enough, my father was listed as a co-signer on one of the four loans included in the complaint.

I knew that they had the power to garnish wages. As a 1099 employee, it would be impossible for them to garnish my wages. My dad, however, receives social security benefits as he's in his 70's and he works as a bartender. I had no idea how this could affect him.

I'm not sure I can even put into words exactly how I felt in that moment. I was scared, of course. But more than anything I was upset that I had put my father in this position. Because of me, he was now having to deal with the stress of this lawsuit. That pained me immensely. I never wanted to be a burden on my father or anyone. I never imagined that something I did expecting to better myself and create a better future would become the same thing that hurt me for years to come.

You may be wondering how exactly that's possible. Here's my experience –

I went to a private law school for three years. The entire expense (tuition, housing, living expenses, etc.) was all covered by student loans. I never imagined that I wouldn't pass the bar exam. School had never been an issue for me. When I finally passed the bar exam, I had started working for a large company and was making good money. I had no desire to then transition into a job in the legal field. Once I was laid off, I found it hard to find employment due to my law degree. I was either over qualified or too much of a risk.

Apparently, potential employers think that you'll jump ship if something better comes along. The hiring manager at my previous company even shared with me that he was apprehensive about hiring me due to the fact that I may only be seeking interim employment while looking for a legal job.

It's an interesting world we live, isn't it?

Once served with the complaint, I had 20 days to file a response. I wrote up a response on behalf of myself and one for my father to file as well. Then we received our court date. That brought a whole new wave of emotions with it.

I have a tendency to over think, to over analyze, to worry about all the "what if" scenarios when going into a situation where I don't know what to expect. My own insecurities started to overtake me.

I kept worrying about how the judge was going to respond to me or interact with me. I was nervous he/she wouldn't have any sympathy for me since they had gone the same path of law school.

I was worried about the opposing counsel. I didn't know how aggressive he would be.

I was already embarrassed and ashamed of the situation I'd gotten myself into. Now it had become a matter of public record. I had a lot of different thoughts running through my mind.

Three months later we had to appear before the judge. I was thankful the attorney representing the student loan company was appearing by telephone and not in person. The judge did a quick recap of what the complaint said to ensure everyone was in agreement with the accuracy, then asked me to explain what was happening.

More than anything, I did not want to cry. I began to briefly explain the sequence of events that led up to this moment. The judge was very gracious in his delivery of what the attorney wanted and what the attorney could actually get. The judge explained that the state of Florida offers homestead protection over a person's home and some personal items, including a car, which meant they couldn't force the sale of either for the proceeds to pay against the debt. He said if you have a boat or an airplane, things like that, they will have to be sold so the lender could recoup some of their losses. I chuckled and said that I wished I lived such a luxurious life. The attorney said he doesn't go after cars, but he would definitely go after a boat. The judge looked at me and said, "If you don't have anything, he can't collect anything."

The attorney said he would waive the attorney's fees and only ask for the filing fee to be added to the total amount due. He said if things happen to get better down the road, maybe I'd contact him and offer a settlement so he could collect something for his clients.

The judge explained we would have to complete some paperwork that would list all of our assets and liabilities. This would allow the attorney to see what he could possibly force the sale of to recoup some of the lenders money. There was no mention of garnishing wages or anything.

After the judge concluded the hearing, he asked me where I went to law school. He told me he was really sorry I was going through all of this. He felt as though there were too many law schools graduating too many students when there weren't enough jobs to fill. He expressed how education has become a business.

As my dad and I walked out of the courtroom, I felt like such a huge weight had been lifted. Those ten minutes had been haunting me for months. I spent so many nights lying in bed, unable to sleep, worrying about what might happen.

I reminded myself, as I sat down in my car letting out a huge sigh of relief with tears running down my face, I needed to stop worrying about things God has already worked out.

Chapter Six

Faith and hope work hand in hand, however, while hope focuses on the future, faith focuses on the now.
– David Odunaiya

January 2019

During November and December, I made roughly $2,000 each month. I knew that it should increase in January, as that was the busy time of year for my sister-in-law's business. I was excited when my sister-in-law reached out and asked if I could help her with some real estate work. Not only because I wanted the opportunity to use my real estate license, but also because I wanted to bring in additional income.

While it ended up only being an extra $625 spread out over the next couple months, it was more money than I would have had otherwise.

February 2019

I walked out to my garage to head to the store, pressed the button for the garage door to open when suddenly I heard a loud snapping sound. The chain for the garage door had fallen on top of my car.

The chain seemed to be intact, so I thought I could fix it. I called my dad to ask for help, as I couldn't manage to do it on my own. He came to my house and we managed to get the chain back on the wheel, but then the wheel broke off completely. I went on Google to see if I could simply replace the wheel and reattach the chain. My dad told me it wouldn't be that easy as the shaft that the gear is attached to had broken, too.

I looked up the cost of a new garage door opener. It was at least a couple hundred dollars. I told my dad that I would just manually open the garage door until I could afford to replace the opener. It's not like it was a necessity. I could make do.

The next day, my dad called me and said there would be someone coming to the house to replace the garage door opener and he would be by around the same time to pay the guy. I explained again that it could wait. I didn't want him spending more money on me. Quite frankly, I really hate feeling like a charity case, but there's something I try to remind myself in those moments. If you refuse to accept a blessing from someone, you're standing in the way of allowing that person to be a blessing.

We all have a desire to help others. Okay, well, maybe that would best be said as most of us have a desire to help others. It's important to allow someone to help you as much as you like to be the one helping.

The new garage door opener cost $360 installed. Plus, the guy fixed this popping sound that kept happening when the door was opening that I couldn't figure out how to fix. Turns out there was an issue with the roller coming off the track. Now, when I open the garage, you can barely hear it. My dogs don't even realize I'm home until I open the interior door, it's that quiet.

That wasn't the only blessing coming my way during the month of February.

In August of last year, I was having dinner with a friend Alison from church. She mentioned she had registered for the Disney Princess half marathon. I was literally in shock, as I had just been thinking about asking her if she wanted to do a half marathon with me to give me a goal to work towards and help me get back into doing daily runs.

At the time, I had an extra $200 to register so I did while we were sitting at the restaurant. There were supposed to be 4 girls going, so I thought we'd make it a girl's weekend and share a hotel room. A few months prior to the event, Alison told me her husband had reserved a room for them at one of the Disney host hotels where you could catch a bus to the race. I checked the prices and it was close to $200 a night. That just wasn't feasible. I looked at other hotels that were close to $100 and 20 minutes away from Epcot, which was where the race started.

As the race was approaching, I kept thinking to myself things would get better. I'd be able to book a hotel as business usually picks up in January. But with the loss of my network marketing income, I just couldn't swing the added expense.

I had already made the decision that I was going to file bankruptcy. There was just no way I could handle all my outstanding debt. I had already been sued by the student loan company. I expected that there would be other suits to follow.

I had to go to Orlando to file the paperwork with the bankruptcy court, so I decided to wait to file until the day I had to go to Orlando to pick up the race packet. Might as well do it all in one day instead of making multiple trips to Orlando.

I told Alison I was going to pick up my race bib and head back home. I would then just drive to Orlando the morning of the race (which started at 5:30am) and then drive home after. Or, I may not do the race at all because money was so tight.

She said she needed me to do this with her, so she would pay for my gas and food. Let me tell you, it's such a blessing to have friends who are so quick to be generous. At the same time, the old ego rears its ugly head reminding you of what a charity case you are. It's embarrassing for me to still be that friend who constantly has to say no to things because she doesn't have the money. I didn't want to let Alison down or let myself down. I paid the money to do this race. I sacrificed many mornings sleep to prepare for it. I needed to see it through.

A week before the race, a friend from school, coming into town for the race called and told me I could crash in her hotel room since her other friend decided to get her own hotel room. She was staying at the same hotel as Alison, which made it super convenient to not only be able to meet up and all go over to the race on the bus together but also not having to drive over the morning of the race.

Something that had been stressing me out for months – how I was going to come up with the money to be able to go out of town to participate in the half marathon – had all been worked out in my favor. It didn't cost me anything above money I would have spent otherwise. But God wasn't done blessing me yet.

As I was getting ready to leave that Saturday afternoon to go to church before heading to Orlando, my dad pulled up to my house. At first, I was kind of annoyed because he was supposed to take care of my dogs that night for me and he was really early. He walked up and said "I'm glad I caught you" and handed me a twenty-dollar bill. He said, "Here, so you have some cash on you just in case".

If that didn't make me feel like an awful daughter! My first response was annoyance that my dad had shown up early. I've had a lot of moments lately where I find myself having to question the condition of my heart to determine why I react the way that I do. But that topic could be covered in a completely different book, there's so much to talk about.

I went to the 5:00PM worship experience before heading over to Orlando. I was dealing with a lot of different stressors and self-doubt. I wanted to position myself in a way that would allow God to speak to my heart and feel more at peace.

You're probably going to judge me for what comes next, and I can't even really blame you. The friend whose room I was crashing in free of charge, text to tell me that parking was $23 or valet was $33, and I could just Venmo her the money. I stood there looking at my phone thinking, *you're kidding me, right?* All the money that gets wasted on frivolous shopping, and you're worried about $23?

Shameful, right? I literally just went from a place of gratitude to a place of entitlement real quick. It wasn't even that I was now being thankless, but I somehow thought that she should cover my parking fee, too. Unreal.

As I reflect, it upsets me that I didn't remain in a place of gratitude for everything she had already done for me. My problems are not anyone else's problems. My responsibilities are not anyone else's responsibilities.

I'm sharing this with you in hopes that you find it as appalling as I do now. I also hope it causes you to reflect on times in your life when you may have experienced something similar and need to check your heart should you find yourself in a similar place again.

On the day of the half marathon, we all met at 3:30am to take the bus over to the race entrance. The race wasn't until 5:30am, but due to the sheer number of people in attendance (just over 20,000 people!) they encouraged early arrival so you could have time to eat, relax, go the bathroom, and even take pictures with some of the characters. Yes, characters. Did I forget to mention this was a Disney race?

This was my second Disney half marathon, but it had been 8 years since my first. Perhaps growing up in Florida made Disney seem anticlimactic for me. Or maybe it's just my personality type. I loved SeaWorld far more than Disney's Magic Kingdom. However, now I'm not sure how I feel about the whole Orca issue. But that's for another day.

Once we got to the drop off, my friend that I stayed with went to find her other friend. They had purchased the VIP experience and had a separate area for their pre- and post-race activities. Alison and I went off to explore and kill some time.

For all the rest of the participants, they had a concession stand where you could buy water and bananas. I brought a Quest protein bar with me, but I wanted to get a banana for the potassium to help prevent muscle cramping. As we made it up to the front of the line, I saw that it was $2.50 for a banana. A single banana. I'm pretty sure I could buy 12 or more bananas for that cost at Wal-Mart. I decided I would just stick to my protein bar.

As we walked up to the cashier, Alison said, "Get whatever you want, I have my debit card with me, thankfully," so I got my banana after all.

We headed over to the corrals to line up for the race to begin. Sadly, we were in different corrals, so we didn't get to start the race together. I knew that I wasn't going to be able to run at the same pace as either of my friends. I anticipated being probably 30 minutes behind them crossing the finish line.

The race started off well. It was early, so the Florida heat wasn't an issue initially. As I made it to mile 5, my feet were killing me. I had horrible hot spots on the ball of each foot, I knew that blisters were forming, so I decided to walk. I never anticipated there being a chance that I wouldn't be able to finish the race.

Here's a fun fact about Disney races that you might not know. For the half marathon, they require you to finish the race with a 16-minute pace. That's three and a half hours. They have pace trackers referred to as "The Balloon Ladies" who walk a 16-minute mile. If you fall behind them, you run the risk of being swept.

I was coming up on mile 8 when I saw a woman walk by me with a Disney balloon. I looked back and saw two more women coming upon me with balloons. My heart started to race. There were still 5.1 miles to go and my feet were killing me.

In that moment, I questioned whether I could finish. I questioned whether I could stay ahead of the balloon ladies. I questioned whether I just wanted to give up.

I decided to try my best to finish. I started running but kept getting stuck behind crowds of people walking. They were impossible to get through to be able to run. I began running off the side of the road in the gravel or the grass, doing whatever I could to try and stay ahead of the balloon ladies.

Coming up on mile 10, there were a row of buses waiting. I knew what that meant. A sweep was about to happen. I pushed so hard to avoid being swept. There were tears in my eyes from the pain the blisters were causing. I only managed to get ahead of the last balloon lady but that was enough.

As I turned back, I saw all the people still behind me who were about to be swept from the race and told to get on the buses to be taken to the finish line. There must have been six buses that sat 50 people or more. All of those people were going to be forced to finish the race right then.

I really didn't know if I was going to be able to make it another 3.1 miles. There was so much self-doubt. That voice in my head kept telling me I couldn't do it. I wasn't strong enough to push through, that I should quit and admit that I'd been defeated.

During the entire half marathon, praise and worship music was playing through my headphones. As I kept trying to get through the crowd just to keep up with the balloon ladies, tears were running down my face. I started praying. Begging really. Asking God to please give me the strength to push through. *I can't do this without you God. I need your strength to see me through. My feet want to quit so walk for me.*

I fell behind the balloon ladies on four separate occasions. And each time I had to talk myself into believing that I could do it. It was getting hotter and I felt like I was overheating. I had to stop for water at every station.

As we passed through mile 12, I managed to just miss another sweep. I heard the officials say to get ready to pull the orange rope across the road as soon as the third balloon lady passed.

I kept telling myself, *just one more mile, just one more mile.*

I could hear one of the balloon ladies shouting for everyone to hurry up and keep pushing because they did a sweep with only half a mile left during the 10k the day prior. I was struggling – bad! Over and over in my head I kept pleading with God to help me finish. I didn't make it this far to be swept with only half a mile to go.

I looked ahead for the 13-mile banner. It wasn't within sight. Really? How was that possible? This was seriously the longest mile of my life. Then I heard bystanders yelling, just a little more than half a mile left. There it was. The dreaded half mile where people were swept the day before.

And they did it again during the half marathon.

I managed to get ahead of the third balloon lady again and avoid the sweep. At this point, it was literally like a can of sardines. We were all so squished together trying to push forward. Whenever I could find an opportunity to try and run around people, I would. I wanted to be done. I needed to be done.

Everyone that was left walked through the finish line because it was impossible to run. I was literally one step in front of the last balloon lady, but I did it. I finished and all I could say was *thank you, God. Thank you for seeing me through. Thank you for helping me overcome. Thank you for your faithfulness.*

You see, in that moment, I realized that everything I've been through these past few years has increased my belief in God's ability to show up in the moments I need him the most. If I asked, I would receive. It's not just about trusting God with your finances. It's about trusting God in all areas of your life.

No one knows more than I do how easy it is to let the devil get in your head and make you think that God won't show up for you because you're not worthy. You are worthy, friend. You are deserving. You are loved. Unconditionally loved by God. Please don't ever forget that.

Once I crossed the finish line, I found Alison with her family. They were all hanging out waiting for me. After eating the snacks provided once you cross the finish line and taking some time to rest, we walked over to the buses to get back to the hotel. I have never been so excited to shower.

As I was relaxing with my friend from school and her mom back in the hotel room, I got a text from Alison. Their bag was left on the bus with their car keys in it and they were trying to track down the bus driver in hopes of getting their belongings back. Her husband decided to stay another night in Orlando, but their oldest son needed to get back home for school the next day. She asked if I could give him a ride since I was planning on leaving shortly to head home.

Remember when I mentioned how I hated feeling like a charity case and much preferred to be the one who is able to help someone else? I now found myself in a position to be a blessing to the person who had blessed me so much already during the course of this weekend. I was happy to be able to help.

There was more to come during the month of February. I know you're going to find it incredibly hard to believe that even after all of God's faithfulness, as I sit in this moment writing this, I still struggle to have peace in this season.

For the last two months, I've been diligent in reading my daily devotionals, doing my scripture writing, writing five things I'm grateful for each day, and writing positive affirmations. One of the devotionals I read is Jesus Calling by Sarah Young. Day after day, I would read these pages aloud with tears running down my face. The way the book is written is as if Jesus is speaking to you. I read it out loud so that I can hear the words as they're being spoken to me. It's powerful.

On February 22, one of the scriptures was John 16:24. "Until now you have not asked [the Father] for anything in My name; but now ask and keep on asking and you will receive, so that your joy may be full and complete." (New International Version)

As I read this scripture out loud, I had tears running down my face. I stopped and prayed. I told God that I needed a miracle. I needed help. I needed more money. I asked in Jesus name not knowing how it would happen. Feeling hopeless.

But God. Won't he do it.

The next day I decided to check my mail to see if I had received anything from the bankruptcy court yet. They told me they would notify me of what else was needed and I would have 14 days to get it turned in. The only mail I had was two envelopes from my mortgage company.

I assumed that one was my monthly statement and the other was the modification application that I had requested. My hope was that the bankruptcy would be approved, my debt discharged, and debt to income ratio would finally fall to the range that would allow me to get my mortgage modified.

I opened the thicker envelope. It wasn't an application for a loan modification but my annual escrow analysis report. As I opened up the legal-size paper that was folded into 4 parts, I see at the bottom a check for $554.

I immediately called my mortgage company to see if it was a mistake. It wasn't. They over estimated what my escrow account would need for the year and by law they had to return the overage to me.

Not only did I get a check for $554 but my loan payment was also being reduced by $50 a month starting the following month.

I sat down and started to cry as I thanked God for his faithfulness. I had no idea where extra money could possibly come from but if I had to guess, my mortgage company never would have been even a remote possibility.

I want you to know that just because you have God moments, it doesn't mean you won't then also have moments of doubt.

It hadn't even been a week I found myself anxious. Nervous about money. Nervous about the pending bankruptcy. Nervous about how I was going to pay for all of the pending bills from the $330 I needed to have the 30,000 mile service on my car, the $450 for my real estate license and association membership dues, the $200 HOA dues, the $365 bar license renewal fee, etc. All of this on top of my existing monthly bills.

It is so easy to feel hopeless. To allow these things to overwhelm you.

As I laid in bed, I had a moment where I remembered that I had the power to control my thoughts. I may not be able to quote scripture or tell you the book, chapter and verse where to find it, but I do know what God's word says.

I started rebuking the devil in Jesus name, telling him that he had no place in my thoughts and he had to leave. I proclaimed God's grace and goodness over my life. I started quoting the parts of the bible that I did know, like God using all things for the good of those who love him. I spoke peace over my life, my thoughts, and my heart.

When you call on God, he will ALWAYS show up. Having spent hours lying awake consumed with worry, it only took minutes for me to fall asleep after I declared the word of God over my life.

I know I'm not the first person to tell you the importance of staying in God's word. This is exactly why. You can't call on the word of God unless you know the word of God. I am living proof that you don't have to be a master of the word; you don't have to have it memorized, you don't have to be able to quote it word for word, line by line. God knows your heart.

God will meet you right where you are.

The next morning when I woke up, I went downstairs and sat at my dining room table to do my morning scripture writing and devotional. The scripture, Matthew 6:31-34.

> "So do not worry, saying, 'What shall we eat?' or 'What shall we drink?' or 'What shall we wear?' For the pagans run after all these things, and your heavenly Father knows that you need them. But seek first his kingdom and his righteousness, and all these things will be given to you as well. Therefore, do not worry about tomorrow, for tomorrow will worry about itself. Each day has enough trouble of its own."

As I moved onto my devotional, the first line read, "When something in your life or thoughts makes you anxious, come to me and talk about it." As I continued to read, I was in awe of how God uses what we're already doing, where we are already, and who we're already surrounded by to communicate with us. The verses from today's reading:

> "Now may the Lord of peace himself give you peace at all times and in every way. The Lord be with all of you." 2 Thessalonians 3:16

> "Do not be anxious about anything, but in every situation, by prayer and petition, with thanksgiving, present your requests to God." Philippians 4:6

> "Come to me, all you who are weary and burdened, and I will give you rest. 29 Take my yoke upon you and learn from me, for I am gentle and humble in heart, and you will find rest for your souls." Matthew 11:28-29

If you haven't read through the Jesus Calling devotional, I encourage you to do so.

Friends, I am literally taking you on this journey day by day with me. Yesterday, I sat on my couch talking about the importance of going to God when you feel anxious. It wasn't but a few hours later that I found myself right back in a state of anxiety.

I received a notice from the bankruptcy court that my request to have the application fee of $335 waived had been denied. The court felt I was able to make monthly payments in the amount of $110, $75, $75, $75. I was so relieved when I received the check for $554 that I was going to be able to get the 30,000-mile service done on my car that was 12,000 miles past due for $350.

I actually sent a text to my boyfriend at the time telling him that I don't want to write anymore because every time I start, my faith gets challenged again. In my heart I know it will all work out. I just wish I had a little more time in between the moments when I have to sit and remind myself over and over again.

Chapter Seven

To trust God in the light is nothing, but to trust him in the dark – that is faith.
– C.H. Spurgeon

I wish I could say it was easy for me to trust God without any fear or anxiety ever entering my heart. But that would be a lie. I often worry about how things are going to happen instead of focusing on who is going to make things happen.

I have fallen out of my morning routine. I had been getting up at 6:30am to go for a 3-mile run then coming home to do my devotional, scripture writing and positive affirmations. But lately, I struggle just to get out of bed. Some days, that doesn't happen until almost 10am. I started reading the First 5 devotional while lying in bed so it's not all bad.

On the morning of March 23rd, I got up, went downstairs and decided to read my Jesus Calling devotional. I had to catch up on a couple days. When I got to the devotional for March 23rd, I read, "I am a God of both intricate detail and over-flowing abundance. When you entrust the details of your life to Me, you are surprised by how thoroughly I answer your petitions." (Young, 2004)

After I was finished reading, I started praying. Sometimes I feel silly praying due to the redundancy of my prayers. I kept praying about my finances as if God doesn't already know exactly where I'm at. That's when I have to remind myself that God wants to hear from me. It doesn't matter how many times I come to him with the same burdens. He wants to be my refuge.

Despite my own sense of silliness, I prayed again and I would have to keep praying to get through. Life doesn't get any easier. We just get stronger. Isn't that what they say?

A couple days later, I got a call from my dad's girlfriend. She wanted to have his house cleaned before they arrived back into town as they had company coming over the very next day and wouldn't have time to do it themselves. Instead of hiring someone off the internet, she asked if I would do it for $300. I was more than happy to have the opportunity to earn more money.

On the 27th, I had a meeting with the bankruptcy trustee. It was scheduled at the bankruptcy court in Orlando. As I was driving there, I had a total God moment. It started pouring down rain to the point where you couldn't see the lanes to drive in.

My anxiety was already high. I was nervous about the meeting. I didn't want to be late. I was also nervous about getting lost because I hate driving in Orlando with all of the construction and not being able to tell where you're supposed to be going based on GPS. And now I was worried about being soaked.

As I was driving, I kept being reminded of Matthew 17:20 where Jesus said, "Because you have so little faith. Truly I tell you, if you have faith as small as a mustard seed, you can say to this mountain, 'Move from here to there,' and it will move. Nothing will be impossible for you." (New International Version)

Did I have enough faith to make it stop raining? I needed the rain to stop so I spoke, "I declare in the name of Jesus that this rain is going to stop. I rebuke you Satan. You have no place here. This rain will stop."

Not even 5 minutes later, the rain let up. Thank you, Jesus! It was just a light drizzle as I walked to the building where my meeting was. I said to myself "so does this mean I don't have faith since it's still raining? Although, it did drastically stop so I'm going to take that as a sign." The umbrella was enough and I was perfectly dry walking in, and on time.

But God - won't He do it!

As I walked into the court house, the security guards explained that the meetings had been moved up to the 6th floor into courtrooms A or B. I was confused why my meeting with the trustee would be in a courtroom. I thought it was a personal, one on one meeting. It was not.

I walked into the courtroom and there had to be between 20-30 people sitting there waiting. I found a seat and watched as people's names were called and they had to go before the trustee to answer a series of questions. Some people had their attorneys with them. Some were alone, like me.

I was really surprised how many mistakes the attorneys made on the paperwork. It was obvious that the trustee was not pleased. If I had paid someone $1500 to complete my paperwork for me and handle my bankruptcy, I would expect them to know the process and read over the paperwork prior to submitting it.

The trustee asked one of the attorneys how they determined the value of the vehicles and the attorney responded they used the Kelly Blue Book value. She corrected the attorney as that is not the method that the courts use to determine value and they should know better. My heart got a little tight. I used the Kelly Blue Book value for my car. Uh oh.

An hour had passed since my meeting time and I still had not been called. I realized the cases were being called in order of filing. I was counting down to my case number when the trustee decided it was best to do all the Spanish speaking meetings at once since she had to call a translator to conduct the meeting for her.

I understood why this made the most sense, but dang. Sitting through these 4 different cases was brutally painful to listen to. I remember when I worked as a representative on the phones for a bank, we had to call the language line any time we had a caller who did not speak English. The calls could last for an hour or more depending on the complexity.

Once she finished those cases, she needed to take a break. I couldn't blame her. I would want to step out of the room to clear my head too. And since I was next to be called, I was more than happy to let her take some time to herself.

She walked back inside, sat down, pulled up the next case and called my name. My heart started to race. I prayed that she would just run through the questions and I would be done in 5 minutes.

As I sat down, she greeted me with "how's it going?" which I was not expecting as she hadn't greeted anyone else while I was there. I smiled and said, "it's going". I wondered if she remembered me from when I called her to get clarification on the documents needed. I explained how scared I was that I was going to mess up and wanted to make sure I did everything correctly.

The first step was being sworn in. She asked me to raise my right hand as she recited "do you swear to tell the truth, the whole truth, and nothing but the truth." – 'I do". Yes, we've taken God out of the court system but that's a discussion for another day.

As she placed my paperwork in front of her, I could see a lot of notes written down and I immediately became nervous. She went through the series of questions prior to addressing her concerns on her notepad.

She asked me if I owned any jewelry as I did not answer it on the paperwork. Oops. No, no jewelry.

She explained that in the state of Florida, you can have unlimited equity in your homestead property, which is protected. But you are only allowed $1,000 in personal property and I had listed more than that but not by much so she was willing to let it remain as is. Then she brought up my car. I said, "I used the Kelly Blue Book value too. I'm sorry, I didn't know that was wrong."

"You're not a lawyer. She was. She should know better. You wouldn't." I smiled inside a little.

My internal smile quickly went away as she explained to me that I could only have $1,000 in equity in my car. I currently had $2581 in equity. The one time when Honda holding its value didn't benefit someone.

If I wanted to keep my car, I would have to buy it back essentially by paying the trustee $1581, which would then be distributed to my creditors accordingly. With $550,000 in debt, I wanted to laugh at the thought that she was going to have to divide up $1581 but that's the way it works, I guess.

I had two options, I could pay the $1581 in full within 45 days or I could pay it over 10 months by making $158 payments starting in 45 days. Here's the catch. The longer it takes to pay the $1581, the longer the bankruptcy stays active. The trustee explained that it would take 3-4 months once the payment had been received in full for her to distribute it and the bankruptcy be closed.

This is where I started to panic and based on how she responded to me I'm guessing she could tell as much.

The trustee looked at me and put her arms out on the table in front of me and said, "I'm not challenging you on your figures. I'm accepting them as is. And think about it this way, it's a lot better than having to pay all that other debt, right?"

I didn't really understand what she was trying to tell me in that moment. When I got home, I looked up what the value would be if I had used the court's method. The value of my car could have been $2,000 more than what I listed. She saved me from having to pay an additional $2,000 by accepting the value I entered on the paperwork.

When you start looking, you'll see God blesses you in so many ways that you could easily miss or oversee if you're not paying attention. I had been blessed by the trustee's generosity and I was not going to allow myself to be upset over the $1581 I had to come up with, but that was hard for me.

Here's why. I need the bankruptcy to be completed as quickly as possible. Work had slowed down and I wasn't sure if I was going to be able to pay my mortgage in May. In order to keep my house during the bankruptcy, it has to remain current. My plan was, once the bankruptcy was completed, I was going to apply for a loan modification on my mortgage. With all of my debt discharged, it would drastically reduce my debt to income ratio. Which is one of the biggest factors that comes into play with whether they will approve a loan modification.

I was really hoping to be done with the bankruptcy by May as I read it typically only takes 90 days in the state of Florida. These are the moments when it is so important to reflect back on what you know about God. A sermon entitled "Frustrated Faith" by Pastor Jeremy Foster came to mind where he shared how God isn't going to give us a life that doesn't still require us to rely on him.

I spent the next two days thinking a lot about how I needed to come up with the $1581 as soon as possible. I started looking online to see if there were any jobs at Walmart to stock shelves at night. I needed something to bring in extra income.

I considered asking my brother if he would give it to me and in return I would help them by watching their animals for free when they went of town for horse shows. Honestly, though, I didn't want to do that because then I wouldn't feel as though I could get a regular job because I wouldn't be able to take the time off. With the way things had been going, I had no idea what the future held and I suppose I really just didn't want to limit myself in any way. That may be the smartest or dumbest approach. Time will tell.

I had no idea where the thought came from other than it was a prompting by the Holy Spirit. Remember when I shared about the stocks my dad bought for me as a baby? There had been 50 shares that were part of a stock certificate that I hadn't cashed out because I couldn't find the certificate. I searched for the certificate at my dad's house but couldn't find it. He had no idea where it could be. At the time, I was super annoyed and frustrated but I left it alone.

Since then, I had been receiving quarterly checks that were less than $20 for my earnings on those 50 shares. Several months ago, I changed it so the earnings would reinvest to buy more stock.

Two days after the meeting with the Trustee, I thought about those stocks and decided to log into my account to see what the value was. Current value was listed at $1631. I may have gasped a little.

I called their customer service line, explained my situation and asked for help on where to go from there to be able to sell those shares. The representative was really nice and explained they could reissue the certificate for $75 and then I could sell them. A quick subtraction showed there was only a $25 difference between how much I needed for the trustee, plus the $75 for the certificate, and the amount the shares were valued at. I'm sure there will also be a fee once it's sold so let's say it's going to end up costing me less than $100 to keep my car as opposed to the $1581 I expected to pay out of pocket.

The representative explained the timeline to me. It would take 10-12 business days for them to process the certificate replacement and update the system with the necessary changes. Then it would take another 3-5 business days to process the sale.

Okay so worst-case scenario, it would be 17 business days. It was Friday, March 29th when I spoke to the representative. I mailed the form with the $75 check on Sunday, March 31st. The 17th business day would be Tuesday, April 23rd and the money was due by May 15th, so I was happy.

The next day I drove to the airport to pick up my dad's girl-friend. As I dropped her off at my dad's house, she handed me $40 as a thank you for picking her up and to cover gas. I know it's not a lot of money but $40 was a huge blessing in my book. I would have done it just because, so for her to give me money to cover gas and such was a nice surprise.

When you focus on all the ways that you receive blessings and abundance in your life, you start realizing how often it actually happens.

April 2019

When you see God moving in your life in such a powerful way on a regular basis, you want to take advantage of the opportunities you're presented with where you can be a blessing to someone else. I may not always be able to help people with their needs, but when I can, I will.

I was scrolling through Facebook when I saw a friend's post about how she was working three jobs this week and had tried to find a dog walker to let her dogs out twice a day but it was going to cost her more for the dog walker than she'd make between all three jobs. Knowing this pain all too well, I messaged her and asked where she lived. If it wasn't too far, I was more than happy to help her. Turns out she lived less than 10 miles away.

I told her I was happy to help. She asked me how much I wanted and I told her, just cover my gas and I'm good. I didn't put a price on it. I figured if money was really tight and she could only afford $10 or $15, then I'd still help. I know how hard it is when you have big dogs. She has two Saint Bernard's that are less than two years old. I think one is less than a year old. Having a rottweiler, I know what it's like to have a dog that weighs almost as much as an adult but is clumsy, excitable and just overall high energy.

She needed me to go twice a day on three different days. The first day, I walked in and she had left $25 on the counter for me. I was blessed while being a blessing.

Oh, remember that $300 that my dad's girlfriend paid me to clean my dad's house? That allowed me to get my car serviced finally. It was supposed to be serviced at 30,000 miles but my car was at almost 45,000 miles.

Based on the conversation I had with my mechanic during my last visit, I was expecting it to cost roughly $350. When the mechanic called to let me know the service was done, he told me that they found an issue. I know I can't be the only one whose heart drops when a mechanic says that. Nothing is ever cheap when dealing with a car.

I needed a new battery. He explained the battery was outputting less than half the power it should. He said I could probably put it off 3-4 weeks if I had to. In my mind, I was thinking the battery was going to cost $60-$75. It's been years since I've bought one but they couldn't be that much, right?

I said, "can you tell me what I owe now and what I'd owe if you replaced the battery?"

He says, "you're currently at $301 and a new battery will cost $180."

What the HECK!?!? When did batteries get so expensive?

After the initial shock subsided, I started thinking. Ok so I expected to pay $350 so it's basically $130 more.

Are you ready? The next few minutes were all God.

I see my upline for the second network marketing company that I joined (did I mention that, I can't even remember at this point I've shared so much of my life with you) post on Facebook that it was payday because the 7th falls on a Sunday. I log in and it shows nothing had been deposited. I wasn't worried about it as it was only $30 anyway so it wasn't a big deal BUT it showed I had $126 on my prepaid card.

There's no way. I know I had that deposited into my bank account last month. I even factored it into how I was going to be able to cover my monthly expenses. I know I did.

I decided to call and check the balance. The automated system confirmed there was $126 on the card. I went as far as to log into my bank account to review the last month's deposits. It hadn't been deposited into my bank account.

I sat there in astonishment. How was that possible? I know I factored that deposit into my spending. I even remembered checking my balance one day and thinking to myself the reason it was so high was because that deposit cleared.

How much was the difference between what I expected to pay and what I would owe with the battery? $130 and I just discovered $126 I didn't even know that I had. Plus, the $30 that would be deposited shortly.

But God. Won't he do it!!

My dad came by to pick me up so we could go get my car from the mechanic. I had called him and told him about the price of the battery before deciding if I wanted the mechanic to do it or if it would be better to try and buy one and do it ourselves. By ourselves, I really mean have my dad do it.

I said to him, "do you want to hear something really cool?" and proceeded to tell him about finding the $126 on the pre-paid card.

There are times when I think that the greatest impact of all God's small miracles is what's being stirred up in my dad's heart. My dad is a believer. He prays. I can't speak to how active his relationship is with Christ. He doesn't attend church but I know that he's watched Pastor Steven (Elevation Church) on television before. I feel blessed and honored that I get to show him a living, active, good God working in my life regularly.

That night he invited me to have dinner with him. As we sat down, he says, "today has been a really great day. I was the first one called back to get blood work this morning, after I went to see my former boss who recently had a stroke and he's doing amazing. Then as soon as I got home the guys pulled up who were there to work on the house. They finished just before you called to go pick up your car, and you being able to pay for your battery… it's been a really great day."

I laughed because I know he was so happy that I was able to pay for the battery and didn't have to ask him to borrow money. He has his own financial struggles and I absolutely hate when mine affect him.

I've found that one of the biggest blessings during hard times are the friends that are always on the lookout for things that may help you. Financial opportunities: babysitting, pet sitting, someone who will pay for a ride. Things like that.

I had shared with friends how I was looking for another work at home job, something in data entry preferably but I had even applied to do telephone customer service jobs from home if it would help bring in some extra cash. Despite having several years of experience on the phone and several more managing those who were on the phone, I couldn't seem to get hired as a freelancer for any of the companies who had posted opportunities.

It's incredibly frustrating when you know you're capable of more but you're willing to do an entry level job because you have bills to pay, yet you can't even manage to get one of those. I'm reminded of one of the candidates we interviewed when I was in corporate America and we were doing a huge hiring for roughly 50 agents. He was older. He didn't really have the experience we wanted with computers or working in a call center environment. But he was a man in need of a job. I felt as though his pride and ego were bruised being interviewed by a woman half his age in a position two times higher than what he was applying for. I voted to hire him. I respected him for taking a chance to secure a position that was, I'm sure, from his perspective beneath him.

I have one distinct memory of him. I don't know how the conversation got started. If it was because something had happened in the news, or because I said something about living alone, but he offered up that both his wife and daughter had taken several self-defense classes as well as gotten their conceal carry permit to legally own and carry a gun. He thought it would be a good idea for me to do so as well. The sincerity in his words and overall genuine concern for my well-being was truly touching.

He ended up quitting before his 90-day probationary period had ended. I'm not sure why, but it hurt me a little. I had taken a chance on him when no one else wanted to, and then he quit. I know that's the concern that most employers have when they see my resume. I won't be a long-term employee. They'll just be wasting the investment to train me and get me up and running in their field.

They wouldn't be completely wrong but I would commit for a minimum of a year if given the chance. If emojis were appropriate in books, I would have ended that sentence with the woman shrugging. Given the trends of our society, I'm sure it won't be too long before it starts happening.

It was April 5, 2019. I received a message from my friend DeeDee on Facebook telling me about a freelance transcription job. I immediately checked it out and started the application process. It was a little intense but with the help of Google, I scored high enough to be admitted to the program. You have a probationary period for the first 100 minutes of transcription. During that time, the goal is to get your work scored at 4.5/5 for grammar and accuracy. If you achieve that, then you advance to the next ranking and it opens the opportunity to choose from more transcription jobs and a raise.

In the first 23 days, I made an extra $275. It is not easy work. It's very time consuming and sometimes exhausting but I was so thankful for the opportunity to bring in any extra money!

Side note: If you're interested in doing freelance transcription work, do a Google search and you'll find there's quite a few different sites that allow you to apply. Don't be discouraged if you don't pass for one of them. They make it challenging on purpose.

On the morning of April 10, 2019, I decided to go sit out on my back porch to enjoy the morning breeze while the dogs wandered around the yard as I worked. I logged in to see if any activity had taken place on the stock account. To my delight, it showed that the stock certificate had been transferred to shares. I was pretty sure that meant I could go ahead and sell them.

I called their customer service line and unfortunately, I didn't get the same representative or one with the same knowledge. The conversation was painful. He didn't understand what I was talking about. He was confused by the paperwork I was referring to. I finally cut him off and said, "Can I sell the shares online now? That's all I need to know." He said, "Oh, yeah, you can." I thanked him for his time and immediately logged back on to initiate the transfer.

When I had originally looked, the value of the stock was $1631. Now, the value was up to $1677, giving me $46 more than I had anticipated! I was so excited. Minus the disclosed fee to have the proceeds direct deposited, I told my boyfriend it was only going to cost me $9 out of pocket to keep my car. Not even 5 minutes later I received a notification on my phone from the Cash App. It was for $10 with a note that said, "Now I bought you your car lol" with a bunch of those laughing so hard I'm crying emojis. I couldn't deny it was funny and a really sweet gesture.

Three days later the funds were direct deposited into my account. I was really surprised when the amount was quite a bit less than I expected it to be. I knew there would likely be a fee but this seemed to be a lot more than that. When I logged onto the website, it was the result of a fee, but for two fees, not one.

Remember how I mentioned there was a certificate for 50 shares and then I had the royalties reinvested since the quarterly checks were for less than $20. It ended up being something like 2.27 shares.

They charged me a $34 fee to sell the 50 shares, and a separate fee of $34 to sell the 2.27 shares, which meant I would be paying $60 out of pocket, not $9. I was kind of upset about it, but I quickly reminded myself that I was still far better off than I would have been otherwise. It's a blessing no matter what.

I went into my office to get my checkbook. Grabbed the documentation for the trustee to include with the check. Looked for the instructions on how I was supposed to make the check out so there's no delays. Look at the amount to confirm there's no cents to be included.

Oh. My. Word.

This whole time I've had the amount of $1581 in my head as the amount owed. Friends, it was $1518! I had received $1596 for the stock. Minus the $1518 for the car and the $75 I had to pay to get the certificate replaced, I made out with $3. If you include the $10 from my boyfriend, I technically had $13 more in my pocket than I did prior to this whole thing. I didn't tell my boyfriend about my math mistake. One, I didn't want to take away from his moment of feeling like the hero. I'm admittedly not very good at making men feel needed so I allowed him to bask in the glory that he "bought my car for me." But even more so, I've become notorious for being horrible at math. Embarrassingly so. It's become a running joke between the two of us. Maybe I'll get lucky and he won't read this and my secret will stay safe.

I was extremely thankful to have that matter resolved. Now the trustee could move forward with finishing the bankruptcy and I could work on getting my loan modified.

I had been praying for more work as much of my income is commission based. Every time I book a new corporate unit, I get a monthly bonus of $100 for as long as the guest remains in that unit. Since we deal with short term corporate rentals, it's not uncommon for the bonus to be for just one, two or three months. If someone books for 4 months or longer, I'm doing a serious happy dance.

Season for us, living in Florida, is typically January through March. That's when a lot of retired couples will come down to the Sunshine State to get away from the cold and snow. This was my first year working for my sister-in-law during season. Based on the prior year, we had both expected it to be really busy. However, in 2019, we only booked about half the units of the year prior. In April, I had three units vacate, three more scheduled for May, and four units scheduled to vacate in June. That left me with only 3 units occupied.

While the notices to vacate kept coming in, I refused to allow myself to get upset. I knew that God would provide. I started praying, asking God to bring six new bookings in the month of May to make up for the three lost in April and three leaving in May. By now you would think I would have learned not to ask only for what I need or limit God with my own limiting beliefs.

We booked two units a day or so after I had prayed. Don't you know that they were both 30-day bookings starting the first week of May. I literally laughed out loud and said, "Okay, God, I see you. I asked for May and I got May. I'm not going to complain they're only for 30 days. I'm thankful and grateful for the $200."

I changed my prayer after that. I started acknowledging the goodness of God and reciting the Ephesians 3:20-21 prayer. "Now to him who is able to do immeasurably more than all we ask or imagine, according to his power that is at work within us, to him be glory in the church and in Christ Jesus throughout all generations, for ever and ever! Amen."

I don't want to limit God or his continued blessings due to my self-limiting beliefs. One thing I know for certain, I cannot even comprehend what God is truly capable of. It's impossible for me to wrap my human mind around it and because I am able to recognize that, I have the power to change my words and my expectations of God.

I no longer want to simply replace what was. I'm asking and believing that God will do immeasurably more than I can imagine.

I get paid every other Friday. In order to help my sister-in-law, I update an Excel spreadsheet that lists what active bonuses I'm being paid on and what bonuses have been closed out. The Wednesday prior to pay day, I go in and update the Excel file to ensure it's accurate. Once I'm done, I send her an email so she knows and can mail my paycheck.

I logged in and pulled up the spreadsheet, then began updating the dates for when each unit was being vacated based on the notices we received. I then added up what to expect my May check to be; it would just cover my mortgage but not be enough to pay other expenses. I saved the file and said, "Everything is going to be fine. I know that God is in control." I didn't allow myself to become upset, but instead had total peace about it.

But God. He will show up and show off when you trust in Him.

Not even an hour later, I received an email that we had a new booking for a three month stay with the option to extend in Orlando. I mention the unit being in Orlando because that means I'm responsible for setting it up and breaking it down, which I will get paid for in addition to the monthly bonus.

When we book units on the west coast of the state, my brother handles the setup and breakdown.

When I stopped trying to limit God with my own expectations, I allowed him to bless me more abundantly.

The very next day, I booked another unit. We also had one client ask to extend through June 1st, which had previously had a vacate date of May 8th. That's 5 of the 6 units I asked God to fill for the month of May. All in the first half of April.

I know we hear about how awesome God is during church. We hear about his goodness and faithfulness. We hear about how God's timing is perfect. Perhaps it's just me, but in the past, when I've been going through some hard stuff, it's hard for me to focus on those things. The longer I'm in the thick of it, the harder it is to trust that God's timing is perfect.

Perfect timing in our minds would be alleviating the struggle almost immediately. Perfect timing would be getting a job within 30 days so none of my bills become past due. It's hard to trust that God's timing is perfect.

> "But do not forget this one thing, dear friends: With the Lord a day is like a thousand years, and a thousand years are like a day." 2 Peter 3:8 New International Version

Chapter Eight

There are certain life lessons that you can only learn in the struggle.
— Idowu Koyenikan

I can remember lying in bed at night, crying, asking God why. Why am I still going through this? Why am I still struggling? Why am I still not able to pay my bills with ease every month?

In those moments, I'm often brought back to Joyce Meyer's sermon during Code Orange Revival. She shared how God kept her in various seasons until she fully learned the lesson that God was trying to teach her through those hard times.

Being completely transparent, I couldn't comprehend what lesson I still needed to learn when I had been faithfully tithing for the past two years. What more could I possibly have to learn? Had I not proven my trust?

Friends, something profound happened in my life between March and April of 2019. I can't put my finger on anything specific that I could pinpoint and say, "That! That was the moment." There were no fireworks. There were no signs in my front yard. There was no friend slapping me in the face.

My heart just changed.

The best way to understand the magnitude of this is for me to go back and tell you a little more about where it started.

There aren't a lot of moments from my childhood that I remember with great clarity, or at all for that matter. However, there is one memory that is still pretty clear 30 some years later. It was the first time I experienced unexplainable, uncontrollable, unrealistic anxiety.

I don't know exactly how old I was but based on my dad's best recollection, I was somewhere between four and six years old. My dad was selling insurance. He worked for this woman, who I still remember her name and what she looked like. She was nice and let my brother and I hang out at the office if my dad ever needed us to.

My memory is of her car in our driveway. She was standing behind the open, driver's side door. My dad walking with his suitcase to the passenger side. My mom standing in front of the car holding my hand as I'm crying, while he tried to reassure me he would just be gone for the night. In my mind, all I saw was my dad getting into a car with another woman with a bag of his belongings in hand.

Why a four to six-year-old would immediately fear that their father was leaving their family for another woman and never coming back, I have no idea. But I was in a state of sheer anxiety and fear until my dad came home.

I know anxiety is a word that gets thrown around a lot. I decided to dig a little deeper into what the actual definition is. According to The Google, I always say it like that because it makes me laugh. We treat Google as an official source so it seems appropriate, but I digress. When I searched "anxiety" on Google, the following popped up: "Intense, excessive, and persistent worry and fear about everyday situations. Fast heart rate, rapid breathing, sweating, and feeling tired may occur. Common causes of this symptom: Anxiety can be normal in stressful situations such as public speaking or taking a test. Anxiety is only an indicator of underlying disease when feelings become excessive, all-consuming, and interfere with daily living." Google states that the source of the information is The Mayo Clinic and other sources.

If you asked people close to me if I suffer from anxiety, some would tell you they've never met anyone with so much anxiety. It's all consuming. I worry about everything. Try to plan every detail. Want everything perfect. All in an attempt to control my environment whereby controlling my anxiety. I believed that if I could make everything perfect, then I wouldn't worry as much. Obviously, that thought process doesn't make a whole lot of sense. One only intensified the other.

I was a "worst case scenario" type of person. My mind always went to the worst possible outcome. Let me tell you friends, this is an awful way to live.

I can remember walking through Wal-Mart one day feeling overwhelmed with not knowing if I could afford to pay for work I needed done on my house, looking at my groceries thinking maybe I don't need most of this. The tears started to run down my cheeks, my breathing labored, I started to gasp, grabbing my chest. It happened so quickly. I was embarrassed that I'd had a panic attack in the middle of Wal-Mart.

This older woman came up to me. She didn't know me and had no reason to be kind to me. She put her hand on my back and said, "I don't know what you're going through but it will be okay." Almost immediately the tears stopped as she just walked away. I didn't get a chance to thank her, or say anything at all. God sent a perfect stranger to be a source of comfort in that moment.

The more I worked towards growing my relationship with Christ through prayer, reading my bible, and scripture writing, I started to almost feel guilty for the anxiety I experienced. I knew that it wasn't from God. I knew the simple fact that I was so consumed with anxiety was evidence I had not yet fully come to accept just how powerful God was. I had not accepted that Jesus' final act of obedience, sacrificing his life on the cross, truly did set me free. Free from shame. Free from guilt. Free from condemnation. Free from anxiety. Free from depression.

Please hear my heart in this. I am not judging you for having anxiety. I am not telling you that you don't trust God. What I am telling you is that for me, personally, my anxiety did not go away until I truly started trusting God wholeheartedly with my circumstances. It wasn't until my faith had grown through crisis after crisis that I was able to learn what it really meant to let go and let God. As my friend Marisol has said, it wasn't personal, it was purposeful.

Pastor Steven Furtick shared a profound word on Easter Sunday (April 20, 2019) entitled The Potential of Pain. He compared what our hope is like as new believers to a plastic egg used for Easter egg hunts: bright, pretty, plastic and hollow. Your hope as an experienced believer is more like that of a hardboiled egg. It has been through the pressure; it has gone through the process. It may fall, it may crack but what's on the inside is still good. It still has value.

You find a new kind of hope on the other side of experience. This is where I find myself now, after having been under the pressure I've felt throughout this financial crisis. All of these experiences have not only grown my faith but my character as well. I have grown as an individual.

If you would have told me five plus years ago that I had so much opportunity for growth, I don't think I would have been open to hearing it. I couldn't see my shortcomings as a person when I was on the top of the mountain. If anything, being on the top of the mountain was proof who I was as a person. It defined me.

Nothing is more humbling than looking at TimeHop or Facebook Memories to see just how far you've come since your time on the mountaintop. I'm ashamed of how judgmental I was of people who were facing hard times. It's so easy to judge when you've never experienced those things in your own life. You think you know how you'd act, how you'd handle it, what you would do. The truth is. Nothing can prepare you for it.

There are some things we know with absolute certainty in this life. One of which is that we will continue to face challenges. There is nothing easy about life these days. I can't speak to earlier generations. It's easy for us to think that life was easier when there was no internet, when things moved slower, etc. My guess would be those living during that time had their own daily challenges they faced.

It can feel as though you have little to no breathing room between one challenge and the next. I will be proud of myself for not allowing anxiety and fear to creep in one moment, but then something else happens and I have to remind myself of God's goodness.

I'm sharing so many details of my life with you because I want you to understand your need for Jesus will never end. Your faith will be tested regularly, if not daily. More importantly, I want you to be encouraged that with each test, each challenge, each struggle you face, your faith grows. The amount of time between when you hear that news and when you experience peace is continuously reduced. You will get to a point where your peace cannot be shaken. The devil has lost all his power to plant seeds of doubt, laced with fear and anxiety.

Now when I find myself lying in bed some nights crying it's not because I'm upset. I am literally overwhelmed with gratitude. I am so thankful for the person I'm becoming throughout this process. I don't know that I could even put into words what it feels like to see God moving and working in your life and on your behalf. To know that God hears your prayers is one thing, but to see him answer them so quickly is life changing.

I can remember times when I would look at other people and see the anointing on their life or the obvious relationship they had with God and wondered how they reached that point.

When Pastor Steven opened his sermon on Easter Sunday, he said something that really resonated with me. He made the statement, "I wonder if Jesus had told them how hard it was going to be, if they still would have followed him?" Really makes you think, doesn't it?

I know when I first recommitted my life back to Christ, there was a part of me that expected because of that decision, because of that step, that life was going to inherently get better. The truth is, it did not. I could write an entire book about expectation verse reality after being saved. Most of us probably could! Can I get an amen?

I certainly did not expect life to ever get this hard. I never thought I would be one of those people who files bankruptcy. The negative stigmas attached to that. The shame. The feeling of failure. But now I understand that this is all just a part of the process, the pressurized process I had to go through in order to come out on the other side of this as the person that God intended me to be.

Please don't think that means now everything is working out and everything is easy. It surely is not.

A week after having received a new booking, I heard back from the community that our corporate application had been denied and we could not lease with their community. It's not common but it has happened once or twice in the year that I've been in this line of work. I didn't think that could happen after we had cleared up some items on the credit report at the end of last year after being denied from another community.

The leasing manager was very apologetic and sent over the business credit report to help assist with determining what might be causing the low rating. To our surprise, Experian still had not updated two matters on the report that should no longer be listed. I was annoyed and frustrated. Yes, when I got that email saying our application had been denied, my heart dropped initially. It did. I was like, come on! But that was it. I didn't even take 5 minutes to pout. It was more like 30 seconds and I was working to find an alternative. I have faith that no matter what, God is going to provide. If this booking falls through, we'll get another one.

In order to try and salvage this booking, I found an alternative community that I hoped would fit their needs. I was hopeful the new community would put their daily rate $15 less than the previous community.

After I sent the email to the agent informing them of the denial and providing an alternative, I sat at my desk and took a deep breath. Reviewing what had just happened in the last 15 minutes and how I responded to the news, I was pleased with myself. In those moments, that's when you know that your faith has grown. Am I perfect? Absolutely, not. Do I have unfettered faith? I wouldn't want to challenge it by saying yes, but I am confident in how far I've come.

I wasn't shaken. I wasn't upset. I wasn't distraught. You may think that's a bit dramatic to say, but the person I was a year ago would have been exactly that. Distraught. Everything was falling apart. Nothing good was happening. It would have been a worst-case scenario response. But not now. Not in this instance.

I never received a response back to the alternative community so I followed up again. The agent seemed confused how this could happen. I never like being in the position to communicate about possible negative things regarding my sister-in-law's company. I don't ever want to make her or her company look bad. I know that word choice is very important. I responded giving a canned response generalizing the how and why. My sister-in-law, who was copied on the email, responded saying it was the perfect response. Again, we waited to hear back regarding the alternative. I followed up again and the agent told me that their client wasn't interested. Bummer!

It stunk, but it didn't change anything. My God is still in control and all things will continue to work for my good!

What's even better than blessings you've prayed about, those you don't! For the past two weeks, I had not eaten out as I had been every other day for the weeks prior. I know, that seems excessive but let me explain.

I'm a routine person. I eat the same things every day for months until I become tired of it and find something else. My current eating routine was a bagel egg sandwich for breakfast/lunch and then Chipotle for lunch/dinner. I get the veggie bowl with chips for $8.94. I only eat half the bowl and eat the other half the next day. So, while I eat out a lot by most standards, I'm not spending a lot to eat out. $4.50 for a meal is better than I could do if I tried to cook it myself. And it definitely would not taste as good!

In my effort to save money or at least stretch money more, I went grocery shopping and bought $65 worth of food. A good portion of which was frozen vegetables or vegan meat alternatives. Mix with some rice and you have a well-rounded meal. It's boring and bland. I missed the flavor of Chipotle but I wouldn't allow myself to go until I ate the food that I had bought.

Out of the blue, my friend Amanda sends me a message and asks if I still use this particular email address. I was caught off guard because that specific email, I only use for DocuSign so that all my confidential information is in one place. I logged in on my computer to check, since it's not synced on my iPhone. There was an email from Wal-Mart. A friend sent you a Chipotle gift certificate. Say what?!

I was so beyond shocked. I thanked her and told her she was so sweet for doing that. It had been sent 15 days prior and I had no idea. She said that I was really on her heart that day and she wanted to do something for me and she thought she remembered me mentioning going to Chipotle before. I laughed out loud for real and told her that it was my absolute favorite so she did really good.

May 2019

Remember my friend who has the two Saint Bernard puppies? I say puppies lightly. They're big! She reached out to me and asked if I could help her during the month of May. She needed me to go once a day, every week day for the whole month. I was more than happy to help again. She asked me how much I wanted to do it. I told her that I would do it for $30 a week. I figured if she couldn't afford that amount, she would tell me and we could go from there, but she agreed.

Again, I didn't want to try and make money off her but I do have to recognize that my time is valuable and it would take 45 minutes to an hour every day to drive there, give them some time to exercise, and drive back.

In life, it's important to remember that you are valuable, your time and energy are valuable.

While I am all for doing favors and helping people out, you can't do those things to the extent that they put a burden on you. For many of us, we have a hard time telling people no. It's even harder to express to someone else a monetary value for your time and effort.

I completely understand that, but I wouldn't be a friend to you right now if I didn't tell you that you have to be just as fair to yourself as you are to everyone else in your life. It's okay to be honest and tell people you're happy to help but you need them to cover the cost of your gas or something along those lines. You have value friend. Don't give yourself away for free.

The first week of May had been hectic! One thing I will say about this business, it can go from absolutely dead to moving 100mph in the blink of an eye. I knew we would start to get busy. I've been telling my sister-in-law for the last two weeks at least that I knew in my heart business was going to pick up. Things certainly looked dismal in March and April.

If you recall, I had been asking God to help us get new bookings for the month of May to replace all the tenants that were vacating. One of the units fell through, so I ended April with only three new bookings instead of the six I had asked for. I wasn't stressing over it though. By this point, I knew better than to question God's timing.

Monday was pretty busy. I had quite a few requests for new quotes. It's not uncommon to quote out a unit and not ever hear back from the guest. There are also times when they'll respond a week or two later wanting to know if the unit is still available. And my favorite, the people who are rush, rush, rush. "I need it now." Only to go ghost after you've gotten everything lined up and ready, then you end up having to contact the community and tell them you don't need the unit anymore. Yeah, those people are gems.

The first of May was a Wednesday. Around 11:30AM, I received an email asking if we had anything in Naples from another corporate housing company that had a client who needed a corporate rental. I started to call a community we always work with to see if they had availability only to find out they were no longer doing new leases with the short-term stipulation we needed to have affordable prices.

I remembered we just had someone move out of a unit on Tuesday at that community, so I looked to see when furniture was scheduled to be picked up. Thursday. It was scheduled to be picked up the next day. I called the community back to see if they had already leased our unit and thankfully, they had not.

I responded to the email letting the company know that we did have a unit in Naples that is scheduled to vacate the next day. I gave them all the specifics: units size, floor level, daily rate, tax rate, etc. In order for us to cancel the furniture pickup and rescind our notice to vacate the unit with the community, I would need a signed lease by 4:30PM.

I figured it would be unlikely that they would move that fast but I was hopeful. The request was for a 90 day stay. Three more months of bonus at a unit we already had, which required little work to flip for the next guest. That's always ideal.

It honestly makes everyone involved happy. We're happy because it's much less work on us. The furniture company is happy because it's one more unit on their inventory they're getting paid on. The community is happy because it's one less vacant unit and they're making money. The new tenant is happy because they're not having to cover some of the extra costs associated with a new setup so their spending less money.

Of course, on this exact day, I not only needed to let my friend's dogs out but then I had to drive 45 minutes north to an appointment to get my eyelash extensions done, then drive home right in the middle of the day. I decided before I left my house around noon to go ahead and prepare the lease for the unit just in case.

I sent the company an email with all the information so they would have it as soon as they were ready to book. I explained

I was going to be out of the office midafternoon and didn't want to cause any delays due to the time crunch we were dealing with. It's nice when you deal with another company, as opposed to the individual themselves who will be living there, because they understand how the business works and more grace is extended amongst each other.

When I left my appointment, I had an email saying they got approval from their client that they were moving forward with the booking but wanted to know the cost to add bi-weekly housekeeping and what the $150 fee was. I explained that housekeeping would be an additional $7 per day and the fee is an exit cleaning fee, which is standard with all of our units. Their client apparently wasn't happy with the $150 fee, so I said that we would waive it. For the next hour, we waited for their client to respond whether or not they wanted to add housekeeping every other week to the terms of their lease.

We were emailing back and forth about how stressful these last-minute bookings are. Like with every business, it's important to build good relationships with the people you work with. Finally, they came back and said they wanted housekeeping. I quickly sent over the new lease as we were coming down to the wire.

Random Side Note: People are funny. They don't want to have to pay for you to clean up their mess after they leave but they're fine paying an extra $200 a month to have someone come and clean up after them so they don't have to live in their own mess. I really have so much respect for people who are in customer facing Customer Service roles. I think I would likely be fired my first day.

She signed the lease at 4:19PM. Talk about a nail biter. I was able to cancel the furniture pickup and rescind our notice with the community. They were happy, we were happy. Everyone's happy!

I almost joked with her; we should do it again tomorrow but decided against it.

I was starting to wonder if I was having premonitions or if I was thinking things into existence.

There's another company that we work with very closely. We get the majority of our new bookings from them. It's also nice that I always work with the same person, who is amazing. She definitely extended me a lot of grace in the beginning when I was first learning the business.

At 2:17PM, I received an email from her asking if a unit I had quoted on Monday was still available. It was another unit that we had on notice with the community, and again, it was scheduled to be vacated the following day. I started laughing and singing, "What a mighty God, what a mighty God."

I called the community and they had not yet pre-leased the unit. I responded back letting her know that it was still available but we had to have a signed lease by 4:30PM to cancel the furniture pickup scheduled for Friday. She responded back letting me know that she didn't think she'd receive a response back from their client today. I was a little bummed but it wasn't completely unexpected.

I decided to go ahead and reach out to the furniture company just to see what our options were. If we canceled the same day pickup was scheduled for, there would be a $215 fee. Yikes! But he was so beyond accommodating. He told me that it was ok if we heard back after 5:00PM, to just send him a text message and he would cancel it so we wouldn't be charged the fee. I passed on the information that they likely wouldn't have an answer today but I appreciate it greatly.

I emailed my contact for the booking back and let her know that there would be a $215 fee if we canceled pickup on Friday. The guest might be willing to pay the fee if they really need the unit. At 4:48PM, she emails me back letting me know they got the okay to book. I immediately sent over the lease, which she was able to sign at 5:11PM. I reached out to the furniture company and let them know we needed to go ahead and cancel and at 5:30PM they responded confirming it had been done.

But God, won't He do it!

I know the corporate housing industry is foreign to most people. I wish I could really impress upon you how rare and unlikely it is that we would have not one but two last minute bookings for units that we were a day away from vacating, then you would really be able to comprehend just how big a role God played in this.

The amount of transparency in these pages is a little terrifying, but it's the thing that scares us the most that often sets us free. I pray as you read about the events that have transpired in my life, you will not only start to find hope in seemingly hopeless situations, but you will have a shift in perspective the way I have.

I had planned to get my hair dyed in early February. It hadn't been touched up since September so it was looking a little rough. Due to personal issues, my friend who has been doing my hair since 2008 wasn't able do my hair. I kept putting it off as I was in no rush and quite honestly, it just wasn't that important to me. But then I put my hair up and saw how many gray hairs were noticeable and decided to reach out to my friend Marisol from church who is a hair dresser. She had blessed me in the past by doing my hair when I couldn't afford it.

I sent her a text message saying, "I have a major ask .. and you can say no!! Is there any way you could put color on my hair? I can pay for the products. I just need it mixed and applied. I can even rinse it myself" and sent her a picture of my hair. She responded, "Oh dang (throw up emoji) roots are for trees hahahahaha."

The timing of reaching out to her couldn't have been more perfect. She let me know that she was actually doing hair Saturday morning at her house. I could come over between 9:45AM and 10:00AM while the other girl's hair was processing. Then she said, "The lowest I can do that for is $35, is that ok?"

While I was hoping that she would do it for just the cost of product, I was quickly reminded of the words I had just written a day or so prior. You have value friend. Don't give yourself away for free. I responded, "That works .. how much is the product" because I recognize her time and talents have value. I knew the product cost was less than $10. I was more than happy to pay for the product and the $35 for her services. She responded letting me know that the $35 included cost of the product.

I told her, "Thank you. Thank you. Thank you." I was so beyond grateful to be getting my hair done. I don't know about you but there's nothing that makes me feel more beautiful and put together than when my hair is freshly dyed. She said, "Oh girl, stop it!!! You know I love you!"

The truth is, I hate having to ask anyone for help, perhaps you can relate. I've spent all of my adult life taking care of things myself. I have tried to color my hair before with store bought box color and somehow, I found it on my clothes, my skin, my shower curtain, the bathroom wall. Needless to say, this is one area where it's necessary for me to ask someone else for help.

It was during the conversation with my friend that I realized we need help from other people. We all do. We weren't meant to go through life alone. God places certain people in our lives during certain seasons whether it be for encouragement, support, guidance, compassion, empathy or love. Your ability to bless someone else is not always dependent upon money. We all have gifts, talents, and skills that God has bestowed upon us that we can use to be a blessing to someone else.

I may not have money to help someone who's struggling financially, but I do have more time freedom than most people who work 9:00AM-5:00PM. When I saw a friend who needed help with her dogs, I gave of my time to be able to bless her. Just as my friend Marisol has a skillset in doing hair, she was able to bless me by coloring my hair for significantly less than I would have to pay if I went to a salon.

We are all brothers and sisters in Christ. God made us for companionship. We are supposed to help each other. God directs us to in his word.

> "Those who oppress the poor insult their Maker, but helping the poor honors him." Proverbs 14:31

> "A generous person will prosper; whoever refreshes others will be refreshed." Proverbs 11:25

> "Those who give to the poor will lack nothing, but those who close their eyes to them receive many curses." Proverbs 28:27

> "If anyone has material possessions and sees a brother or sister in need but has no pity on them, how can the love of God be in that person? Dear children, let us not love with words or speech but with actions and in truth." 1 John 3:17

There should be no shame in reaching out to a brother or sister in Christ during your time of need. God may have placed them in your life during this season to fulfill His promises to you.

"Therefore, as God's chosen people, holy and dearly loved, clothe yourselves with compassion, kindness, humility, gentleness and patience. Bear with each other and forgive one another if any of you has a grievance against someone. Forgive as the Lord forgave you. And over all these virtues put on love, which binds them all together in perfect unity." Colossians 3:12-14

"Two are better than one, because they have a good return for their labor: If either of them falls down, one can help the other up. But pity anyone who falls and has no one to help them up." Ecclesiastes 4:9-10

Pastor Jeremy Foster of Hope City Church shared a message entitled Invisible Prisons of Expectations and said, "You have to be in a group, because you weren't meant to go into the desert alone." Pastor Jeremy had come to Elevation Church to be a guest speaker during our Maybe God series. I would highly recommend watching the whole series on YouTube.

The first week Pastor Steven Furtick preached about how we experience God in the context of our relationships. When we are waiting on God to speak to us, He will often use the people in our lives: family, friends and even sometimes our enemies. You experience God in the context of your contacts. The reason I bring this up is because it's important to be aware of who you are allowing into your life during these seasons of struggle.

As your friend, and someone who wants the best for you, I want you to choose those friends wisely. Simply being a brother or sister in Christ is not enough. Before you allow someone into your sphere of influence, you have to make sure that your expectations of God align. Don't allow yourself to gravitate towards someone who helped you in this season whose motives may not be what they appear. Remember the fable about the wolf in sheep's clothing. It is wise to always be hopeful but cautious.

I realize this might be somewhat overwhelming. I spend all this time telling you about how people can be in your life to bless you and then I divert to talk about how it might not always be what it seems. We can't only focus on the parts of scripture that fit the narrative we want to believe. We have to embrace it in totality so that we can not only have faith and hope but wisdom as well.

> "Do not be misled: 'Bad company corrupts good character.'" 1 Corinthians 15:33

> "Do not make friends with a hot-tempered person, do not associate with one easily angered, or you may learn their ways and get yourself ensnared." Proverbs 22:24-25

> "The righteous choose their friends carefully, but the way of the wicked leads them astray." Proverbs 12:26

You may be wondering, *Well, how do I know if someone should be in my life or not?* I won't lie friends, it's not always easy. There have been times in my life where I allowed people to have far too much influence over me, leading to poor decisions. In my experience, here are some things that have helped me to identify what level of access various individuals will get in my life.

Does their advice align with God's word?

> "If anyone teaches otherwise and does not agree to the sound instruction of our Lord Jesus Christ and to godly teaching, they are conceited and understand nothing. They have an unhealthy interest in controversies and quarrels about words that result in envy, strife, malicious talk, evil suspicions and constant friction between people of corrupt mind, who have been

robbed of the truth and who think that godliness is a means to financial gain." 1 Timothy 6:3-5

This may seem cliché but there is no better way to gauge whether someone is leading you closer to God or away from God.

Now I know you might be thinking things like, *I'm not an expert on the Bible*, or focusing on the fact that you've never read it in its entirety. Have no fear. Go to The Google and do a simple search along the lines of "scriptures that deal with _____." Enter whatever the issue is you're getting advice on.

Better yet. Ask God! His word says, "My son, if you accept my words and store up my commands within you, turning your ear to wisdom and applying your heart to understanding — indeed, if you call out for insight and cry aloud for understanding, and if you look for it as for silver and search for it as for hidden treasure, then you will understand the fear of the LORD and find the knowledge of God." Proverbs 2:1-5

When you ask God for wisdom and clarification, he will answer you. He will give you wisdom. He will give you clarification if you continue to seek him.

Ask God for guidance

When I first recommitted my life to Christ, I struggled with praying. I didn't really know how to pray. It seemed so silly when I was raised in church and my mom prayed all the time. This wasn't something I should be struggling with, but I was. The best explanation I heard, which helped me tremendously, was that God is our father. Just like we have an earthly father, God is our heavenly father. Regardless of whether we do good or bad, our parents want us to feel comfortable coming to them. They want us to talk to them.

> "If any of you lacks wisdom, you should ask
> God, who gives generously to all without finding fault,
> and it will be given to you." James 1:5

> "My son, do not forget my teaching, but keep my
> commands in your heart, for they will prolong your
> life many years and bring you peace and prosperi-
> ty. Let love and faithfulness never leave you; bind
> them around your neck, write them on the tablet of
> your heart. Then you will win favor and a good name
> in the sight of God and man. Trust in the LORD with
> all your heart and lean not on your own understand-
> ing; in all your ways submit to him, and he will make
> your paths straight." Proverbs 3:1-6

What does your gut tell you?

I know you've experienced that feeling in your stomach when
you know something isn't right. It's instinctive. There may be
no rational understanding of it but you trust it anyway.

When I (and you) accepted Jesus Christ into my heart and
into my life, you receive the gift of the Holy Spirit. This isn't
something that comes at a later point in time. The Father, the
Son and the Holy Spirit – they are all one.

> "In Him you also trusted, after you heard the word of
> truth, the gospel of your salvation; in whom also, hav-
> ing believed, you were sealed with the Holy Spirit of
> promise, who is the guarantee of our inheritance until
> the redemption of the purchased possession, to the
> praise of His glory." Ephesians 1:13

The beauty of knowing that you have the Holy Spirit within
you is that you can call upon Him at any time. When you
need help, ask. You can take confidence in knowing that the
Holy Spirit will never lead you astray.

"As for you, the anointing you received from him remains in you, and you do not need anyone to teach you. But as his anointing teaches you about all things and as that anointing is real, not counterfeit— just as it has taught you, remain in him." 1 John 2:27

You have everything you need already within you. God has given you the wisdom you need. You have the instincts you need to know if someone is a good influence in your life. Those that will help you to stay in alignment with God's will.

"And this is my prayer: that your love may abound more and more in knowledge and depth of insight, so that you may be able to discern what is best and may be pure and blameless for the day of Christ" Philippians 1:9-10

The world we live in is hard. Really hard. Quite frankly, I can't even imagine how hard it must be for today's youth. We have to remain guarded, especially of our hearts and our minds. We are flooded with streams of influence all day long between what we see on TV, hear on the radio, see on social media, etc.

"Do not conform to the pattern of this world, but be transformed by the renewing of your mind. Then you will be able to test and approve what God's will is— his good, pleasing and perfect will." Romans 12:2

The people with whom you surround yourself with and spend the most time with will make all the difference in your life. Choose wisely friends.

Chapter Nine

Your transparency will lead to other people's transformation.
–Trent Shelton

When I decided I was going to write this book, I told myself the only way I could successfully convey the true and powerful impact of surrendering control to God and fully trusting him with not just my finances but my future was to be completely and utterly transparent. Not to paint myself as this perfect Christian who made a decision and stuck with it and never faced future challenges.

As I started writing, I also started a business course that Bank of America offered for female entrepreneurs. It's called Cornell Women's Entrepreneurship course. If you're looking to start your own business, you should look into it as it's free and a great way to learn things you may never have otherwise. During the Funding Your Venture and Business Planning course, I started digging into what the costs would be to publish a book. The goal was to fill out this excel with every possible expense so you could be best prepared for what you needed to get started.

I've never written a book. I don't believe that I'm the best person to edit my writing or check the grammar. If I was going to be able to pull this off, I would need help. As I started putting together what would be needed, the expected costs, etc., I wasn't sure that I'd be able to make it happen. I started thinking about a sermon Christine Caine did at Elevation Church in December of 2018 called Don't Drop It, in which she talked about the legacy that we're leaving for future generations. What if this book is my contribution to future generations? This could be how I help others. I couldn't allow the fear of how I was going to be able to pay for it to stop me from writing and publishing this book.

I have had conversations with friends in the past about the various ways they tithe. Not everyone is of the opinion that you should strictly give your tithe to the church. In the Old Testament, there were commands to tithe. God sees tithe as an act of worship. In fact, in Malachi, the people are accused of robbing God by withholding their tithe.

> "Will a mere mortal rob God? Yet you rob me. But you ask, 'How are we robbing you?' In tithes and offerings. You are under a curse—your whole nation—because you are robbing me. Bring the whole tithe into the storehouse, that there may be food in my house. Test me in this," says the LORD Almighty, "and see if I will not throw open the floodgates of heaven and pour out so much blessing that there will not be room enough to store it." Malachi 3:8-10

However, the New Testament does not contain those same commands. In the Old Testament, it was about supporting the Temple in Jerusalem. In the New Testament, Christians are called to support the work of Jesus, which is the building of his church, and to do so cheerfully.

> "The point is this: whoever sows sparingly will also reap sparingly, and whoever sows bountifully must also reap bountifully. Each one must give as he has made up his mind, not reluctantly or under compulsion, for God loves a cheerful giver." 2 Corinthians 9:6-8

Some are of the opinion that your tithe can go to any worthy cause, not just to your local church. I decided that instead of continuing to tithe to my church, I was going to put aside my tithe into a separate bank account to use for the publishing of this book. The purpose of the book is to help God's kingdom, right? Would putting that portion of my income aside for this cause not be valid under the New Testament?

I most certainly was willing to accept that and the opinions of those who agreed that tithing didn't have to go to the church, but could be used in other ways. The last time that I tithed to my church was on March 3, 2019. For the next couple months, I was putting my tithe into savings with the intention that those funds would be used to help publish this book. However, if I'm being completely transparent, there was always a slight nagging feeling in my spirit.

Here's the thing. Like with many things in life, we can "twist" the truth to fit our needs and perspectives when it suits us. There have been people distorting religious teachings for many years to fit their agenda, often political in nature, and there will always be people who tell you that you're doing the right thing because it fits their narrative as well. If we both believe it to be okay, it must be true. Because we are all born sinners, and deception is the devil's biggest weapon, it's not surprising that we are able to deceive ourselves even when we are trying to convince ourselves of what is right.

I sought validation from others that my decision was right, that my choice wasn't out of alignment with God's word. This is when you need people in your life who are more interested in your walk with God than they are in telling you what you want to hear. There will be people who, despite not necessarily agreeing with your decision, will go along with it to avoid confrontation. As someone who is passive aggressive, I can understand the inclination to do this, but by doing so, you're not helping the person coming to you looking for guidance.

I feel extremely grateful and thankful to have a friend in my life who was not afraid to tell me hard truths and not just appease me. I happened to run into her after church and we started chatting. She was asking me how things had been going and I started sharing some of the struggles I've been facing. She and her husband recently started their own company, which I know it took an enormous amount of faith for them to do.

I asked her if I could get her opinion on something. I went on to tell her about writing this book and how I had started putting my tithe aside to be able to cover the costs of publishing it. Without hesitation or reservation, she said, "Tithe always goes to the church. That's what I believe." She went on to share that by giving that 10% to God, I'm trusting that God is going to provide the resources necessary to publish the book, whether it be financing, connecting with the right people, etc.

I shared some of the responses I had received from others who I had asked their opinion on the topic and she was quick to immediately reiterate that what matters is what's said in God's word. If there's no biblical basis, then it's not in alignment with God's word. I knew she was right, but I didn't necessarily believe that I was doing anything wrong.

I tabled the topic in my mind and continued putting the money into savings, despite the fact that I didn't have complete peace about it. Truly, that should have told me everything I needed to know right then.

Fast forward to May 17th. I woke up to an email from Chase with my account balance, just like I do every day, but today it showed $0.00. How was that possible? I had over $100 in the account the day before and didn't buy anything. I logged in and saw that my car insurance auto draft had come out. I completely forgot about it. It showed that $34 had been transferred from savings for auto draft protection. *Good thing I had that money in there* I thought to myself.

I knew I needed to replace the $34 with my next paycheck because that's not what the money was supposed to be used for. As long as I put it back, what was the harm, right?

The following Sunday, I was sitting in church listening to Wade Joy minister to the church in a sermon titled, Stacking Strength, and I knew, without a shadow of a doubt, that I had to go home and immediately tithe the $632 I had put aside for this book.

Wade shared in his message how he struggles with feeling like he's not making a difference in the mundane of daily routine. He went on to share that the lie he tells himself that stops him is that his greatest impact happens when he takes the greatest leaps of faith. But that's not true. His greatest impact doesn't happen through giant steps of faith but in the day to day faithfulness. (Joy, 2019)

Here are some bullet points from Stacking Strength that God used to speak to my heart and give me peace:

Jesus celebrates consistency. Consistency is powerful.

The path of least resistance is rarely the path of obedience.

Peace rarely comes before obedience. Peace is a bi-product of obedience.

Nehemiah 6:16 says, "When all our enemies heard about this, all the surrounding nations were afraid and lost their self-confidence, because they realized that this work had been done with the help of our God." This scripture shows us, teaches us, reassures us that God wants to show others how great He is through our consistent obedience. It wasn't about how strong the wall was that Nehemiah was building, it was about how strong his God was. God built something great through Nehemiah, but what God built in him was even greater.

For months, even before I started writing this book, I knew that it was necessary for me to go through this season of my life in order for me to become the person God wanted me to be. There's no doubt that God has done a great work within me. I'm not even remotely the person I was two years ago, and for that, I am grateful.

After the sermon, as I was walking out of church, I looked up and saw I was walking behind my amazing and beautiful friend Kristin. I smiled because I knew it wasn't a coincidence. I said, "Hey beautiful." She turned around and I said to the guy walking next to me, "See? She knew I was talking to her." We laughed. I gave her a hug and said, remember what we talked about last time, about tithing? She did. I shared with her, as tears started to fill my eyes, how as I was sitting in the worship experience, I knew in my heart that I needed to go home and tithe that money. She commented, "you know it's real (what God was speaking to me through the sermon) because you're getting emotional just talking about it."

On my drive home, I was messaging my best friend Crystal who I had shared all of this with before. As I was talking, there were things coming to light that I may have been sub-consciously in denial about. There was a part of me that liked having the money set aside in savings. It was like a security blanket. I knew that if something did happen, at least I had that money there.

If I was having thoughts like that, it means that I wasn't fully trusting that if something did come up that God would pro-vide. I was still trying to control some aspect of my finances. Yet, if you had asked me the day prior, I would have believed myself that I had overcome these issues. I had grown. I had matured. Clearly, God isn't through with me yet and likely never will be.

It's important to remember that we are only human with a sinful nature. It's easy to feel discouraged when you have moments where you realize that perhaps you haven't come as far as you thought. Don't allow the devil to infiltrate your thoughts. You're not a bad Christian. You're not moving backwards. You are absolutely still making progress. The simple fact that you can identify moments where you've slipped is proof that you're much farther along than you think.

As long as we are here on earth, we are constantly going to face situations and circumstances that will require us to turn our hearts to Jesus. Leah DiPascal said it best, "The process of turning our hearts toward God isn't just a one-time experience when we ask Jesus to be our Lord and Savior…although that turning is by far the most important! Turning toward God happens every day when we confess our hurts, brokenness, disappointments and sinful behavior to Him. It's when we honor and trust the Lord despite our hard circumstances and look to Him for help and restoration. Even if we struggle in the process of turning, Jesus will meet us there with mercy and grace, helping us make the full turn toward God the Father, guiding us every step of the way." (DiPascal, 2018)

It was no surprise to God that I was putting my tithe aside every month into savings. He is all knowing. We are given free will so that we can decide for ourselves, but God is going to use, not just His word, but the people in our lives to guide us in the right direction. It was not by mistake that I stopped and talked to Kristin for so long that evening where I felt comfortable enough to ask for her opinion.

Despite that conversation, I still continued with the same actions for a period of time. If I had wanted to justify my actions, I could have. The reality is, I could read the bible and interpret it based on my own desires, or a basic Google search would turn up articles by self-proclaimed experts validating my choice. Or, I could dig deeper and look for the actual meaning of God's words. I think we've become a society that likes to give big meaning to small quotes; they are often taken out of context and misconstrued.

I found Dave Ramsey's explanation of the difference between tithing and offering to be interesting. "After you've tithed, you can give in other ways: Giving a cash offering to your church above and beyond the tithe, giving money to a charity you support, giving to a friend or neighbor in need, or giving of your time or talents. Not only does giving of your money or other resources generate good in the lives of others, it also generates contentment in your heart." (Ramsey, 2017)

Here's where I landed after reading through scripture. The first 10% should always go to your local church, or the church that you attend as I know many attend churches virtually. If there are other ministries or charities that you want to support, it should be done with monies in excess of your tithe.

I'm not here to judge you if you believe something different. What I am here to do is provide a true and transparent account of what I've experienced in hopes that you will see the beauty in trusting God wholeheartedly.

Chapter Ten

It's all about finding the calm in the chaos.
– Donna Karan

The month of June was such a whirlwind that I decided it best to give it its own chapter. Honestly, I think writing these moments down as they happened has actually helped me. It's allowed me to process everything that was going on while keeping my eyes focused on Jesus and all that He was doing despite feeling overwhelmed and anxious.

June 2019

John C. Maxwell does an excellent job of reminding us of the process we all must go through on our journey to being used profoundly by God. Maxwell says, "God prepares leaders in a slow-cooker, not in a microwave oven. More important than the awaited goal is the work God does in us while we wait. Waiting deepens and matures us, levels our perspective, and broadens our understanding. Tests of time determine whether we can endure seasons of seemingly unfaithful preparations, and indicate whether we can recognize and seize the opportunities that come our way." (Maxwell, 2003)

Remember when my student loan company sued me a year ago? As a result of that law suit, they were granted a judgment against me for the amount of my loans. Even though Florida is a homestead protection state, the bankruptcy trustee told me that I needed to file a Motion to Avoid Judicial Lien on my house and my car, both of which were being released from the bankruptcy under the state's homestead protection laws.

The process was painful. I had to refile the motion 3 times before I got all the wording correct, but there was one blessing that came out of that process. I started emailing one of the clerks in the bankruptcy office who guided me and helped me to get it right. She was gracious enough to put a deadline on my file to ensure that the order granting the motion would be filed by the judge in a timely fashion. I knew that the creditor had 25 days to respond to my motion, so I put a reminder on my calendar to check. Almost two weeks after the 25 days had lapsed and I still had not received the order, so I logged into the bankruptcy court's website to see if it had been filed yet.

I was shocked to see the most recent filing was Discharge of Debtor. My mind started racing.

"Does that mean it's done? But I thought my creditors had until July 29th to respond."

The anxiety started right away too. Along with fear. The biggest unknown during this process was what would happen to my student loans. I had read online that people have been successful in having their student loans discharged through bankruptcy due to financial hardship. My loan originator also told me that she has seen a lot of student loans discharged on credit reports. I didn't know what would happen, but I did know that God was in control and this might be the best way for me to get out from under all of my debt.

That's the whole reason I decided to file for bankruptcy. I knew that God was in control and if others were able to get relief, so could I. The law suit, which was what prompted the conversation with my loan originator because she notarized my documents, would be turned and used for good. That's

God's promise. When I filed the papers, I had full faith in that.

Yet, when I saw the discharge had been issued, faith was not my first response. It was fear. Then there was some guilt. Guilt that my first response was fear, and not faith. Why am I still struggling to fully trust that God is in control? Even if the student loans are not all discharged, God is still in control and there is a plan in place for my life.

To make matters worse, my brother called me to find out what the status was. My brother co-signed on one of my loans and as a result, if I was discharged from that particular loan, he would still be responsible. They closed the account on his credit report, which resulted in his credit score dropping 10 points. He wasn't thrilled about it. I'll be honest, I'm more afraid of dealing with my brother than I am dealing with debt collectors. I explained to him that it's a wait and see game. There was no guarantee that the student loans would be discharged, but it was my best shot to try.

When I got home, I checked my mail to see if the paperwork had come yet. It was five days since the bankruptcy system showed the update so I thought it might have arrived. It hadn't. Instead, there was a letter from a local car dealership saying they offered deals to people who had recently been discharged from bankruptcy. I guess then it's true. The bankruptcy is done.

A couple hours later, I received an email from the company who was guarantor of my federal student loans letting me know that they were in default.

My heart sank. I started to cry. Then I started speaking over my situation. "God is in control. No matter what happens, God is in control. God has a plan for my life. I don't know what that plan is but I trust that God is going to work everything out in my favor."

One thing I have gotten much better at is singing praise and worship music when I feel overwhelmed or thankful. I started singing, albeit not very well, "What a mighty God. What a mighty God you are." Over and over again. I may even make up some of my own words when I can't remember all of the lyrics. I'm thankful for a God who loves to hear us sing, even when we're bad at it.

In this moment, as I type these words, I don't know what's going to happen. Honestly, I expected to have this book all written before the bankruptcy had even finished, but it would seem it's much harder to put everything down on "paper" when you find yourself reliving the emotions of the moments you're writing about all over again. As I was driving the other day, I started crying about something. I can't even remember now what it was, I only remember saying, "God, sometimes I really wish you wouldn't have given me such a big heart. I wish I didn't feel things so deeply, and I would really love to cry a little less. There's so much crying lately."

It's hard to feel emotionally stable lately when everything seems to make me cry. I don't ever remember crying as much as I have in the last couple months. I used to see crying as weakness. I hated crying. I still hate crying in front of other people, but it is certainly not a sign of weakness. Weak is not a word I would use to describe myself. Not even a little.

I have faced battle after battle all on my own with very little support from the people in my life. I don't necessarily blame them for that. I do think people tend to believe that I'm much stronger than I feel I am, and they don't think I need the shoulder to cry on or the comforting hug. I learned when my mom died that I needed to take care of myself, support myself, heal myself, and be there for myself.

What I didn't understand then that I do now is that I'm never alone. I talk to God a lot. Random conversations without any real beginning or end. As if He's in the room with me at all times and there's no reason to announce myself or conclude our time together. I know that whenever I need to talk, He will listen. When I need peace, He will comfort me. It would be nice if I could physically feel a hug, but I'm happy to accept the sense of calm and peace He brings over me.

There are times when I think that chaos happens just to test my response. Will I immediately become afraid or will I stay calm and have peace? Honestly, it depends on the day. But this week has been nothing short of chaos.

On May 22nd, I had informed an apartment community that our client wanted to book a unit they quoted to me two days prior. The leasing consultant I spoke with was off, so the woman who answered the phone was helping me. She sent me the quote for the unit via e-mail and I had to apply through the link. If the application was approved, we could pay the reservation fee. That's the only way they could reserve the unit for us.

I clicked on the link. The only way to apply was as a person, not a company. I tried to call the community back half a dozen times but couldn't get through. I decided to go ahead and apply so we wouldn't risk losing the unit. In my mind, there was no reason why we couldn't get the unit transferred into the business name in time for the guests to move in, which was almost a month later. Days went by and I was unsuccessful getting anyone on the phone at the community. I sent a couple emails, but no reply.

Finally, I forwarded the email I sent the original leasing agent to the second agent that I spoke with. I received a response apologizing for the delay followed by, "I don't think we have a separate corporate application." I responded politely that I would wait for the original leasing agent to return from vacation to get it worked out. In the meantime, I had the application for their management company already on file, so

I forwarded the application, along with the necessary paper-work.

Ten days later I'm told that the application for the business was denied because we didn't have any trade lines on our credit report. Essentially, we needed to have a credit card (or maybe even two) that was reporting to the credit reporting agencies. I told the leasing agent that we have two. I could provide a copy of the statement as well as another trade line that doesn't report if it would help. She said yes, provide the documentation and she would submit it to be overturned.

A week later, I'm informed that they cannot overturn the denial. It has to be listed on the credit report, if it's not, too bad. I ask if we can just leave it in the business owner's name and add the guests as occupants. Again, I'm told they'd work on it but didn't see why not. I hear nothing from the community that leads me to believe that there is any reason to be concerned.

We were scheduled to take occupancy on Wednesday, June 19th. Monday, at 4:30pm I get a phone call from the leasing agent telling me that there's no way to proceed without the guests also being put on the lease, having their credit and background run, and signing it. I was dumbfounded. Here we are, at the 12th hour, and she's telling me that we can't move in on Wednesday?

My heart started racing. My anxiety went through the roof. I asked to speak with the regional manager because there was no way this could happen. We've been working on this for three weeks and not even two days prior you're telling me this is where we're at? I'm told that they can't give out their number but that they will send him an email and he will call me the next day.

I'm on the phone with my sister-in-law. I'm on the phone with my brother. I'm calling the credit card company. I'm mailing letters. I'm looking for an alternative community just in case. My sister-in-law is calling Experian, the credit card companies, etc. We're frantically trying to get this fixed.

Then I stopped. I stood still. I took a deep breath. I exhaled and said out loud, "My God is so much bigger than this." I proceeded to talk to God. I invited God into my situation. There was nothing that God couldn't fix. Whether it was finding another community, Experian updating the credit report, or the community allowing us to proceed with the lease as is and add the guests only as occupants. No matter what, it would work out.

When I woke up on Tuesday, I started calling communities again in the hope that I could find something that fit all the needs of our guests. Experian said the credit report should be updated by Wednesday, but they couldn't make any guarantees. Then the regional manager called. We discussed everything that had taken place from May 22nd until now. He said he was going to see what he could do and would be in touch. I advised that we had furniture scheduled for delivery on Wednesday, and if I had to cancel, I would need to do so by 3:00pm or we would be charged. He said he understood and would try to get back to me as soon as possible.

An hour and a half later, he called me back and told me that we could proceed with keeping the lease as is but we would have to add an addendum that included the guest's names as occupants. Once the credit report was updated, he would transfer the lease into the company name. I was so beyond grateful. I thanked him repeatedly and apologized for being a crazy lady. He was gracious and I was appreciative.

I immediately called my sister-in-law. The first words out of her mouth were, "Please tell me something good." I explained everything that the regional manager shared with me. We were both greatly relieved. Once I hung up the phone, I took a breath and realized I had not yet thanked God for

once again showing up in the midst of my madness to come
through for me.

That was one crisis down.

I made it through the complete chaos from work only to
open my email to find one from ECMC. Educational Credit
Management Corporation. They were now the guarantor of
some of my federal loans. My heart started to race. It was the
usual, these are the consequences of going into default on
your loans.

I did a Google search and found a lot of negative reports.
Some said that the company was a scam just trying to get
your personal information. Others said they harass you nonstop. I didn't know what to believe. I called the number and it
asked for your social security number. I started, then thought
how dumb of an idea that was if it was, in fact, a scam. I
couldn't remember if they even announced the name of the
company when I called.

When I checked my mail, there was a letter from them again.
I recognized the amount listed that they said I owed from
some paperwork when I was doing the bankruptcy application. I went through and found a letter from the previous
guarantor saying that they had transferred the loans to this
company. I previously requested a copy of the loan origination documents, as I had no idea what these loans were, they
said I owed.

I never received the paperwork, so before I gave this company any of my personal information, I wanted to make sure
they were legitimate. There are so many scams surrounding
student loans because it's easy for anyone to access the information online through the national data base. I decided to
wait to see if I got the loan origination paperwork in the mail.

I'm going to jump ahead of the timeline here to finish this particular story.

Over the next week, I continued to receive phone calls and emails from this same person saying they were from ECMC. I was still really apprehensive, and to be fully forth coming, I didn't have any money to pay them so what did it matter anyway.

On June 25th, I received another voicemail and this time they emailed me on my work email. I thought to myself, the stuff I read online is true about this company. Shortly after I got the email, my sister-in-law reached out to let me know they had contacted her on the business line to verify my employment. They were sending her paperwork to start the wage garnishment process. At that point, I decided they must be legitimate if they have the ability to do that through the courts.

I called the number back on the letter but didn't enter my social security number. I used the account number listed on the paperwork. When I finally got through to someone on the phone, the individual who answered was hard for me to understand. I asked to speak with the person who had been calling and emailing me. Thankfully, they were able to transfer me to him.

We started talking and I explained to him I wasn't sure what this loan was that they were referring to in the letter. He told me that he could send me the original origination documents. I must admit, the gentleman helping me was very informed, kind, compassionate, and empathetic to my situation. He went over the different options that they could offer and suggested I do the income-based repayment plan.

I shared how just the day prior I received a letter from Navient, who services some of my other federal loans, about how I needed to reapply for the income-based repayment plan, so I did it online. When I was done, it said that there

was another company that held my loans who didn't participate in the online option and I would have to mail them my
application. The company was a different name than ECMC.
He went onto the national database to pull up all of my loans
and told me that it might be in my best interest to consolidate
all of my federal loans. I immediately cringed. To me, that
meant that I would have one much larger bill to pay than several smaller payments.

Apparently, a couple years ago, the government made a
change to how they determine the payment for the income-
based repayment plans. It was no longer based on how much
you owed and only based on how much you make. Consoli-
dating would allow me to pay just one payment, instead of 3
or 4 for different loans. That would mean that regardless of
the total loan balance, the payment would be the same as
what I qualify for right now, provided my income doesn't
change.

Their program is designed where after you make 10 monthly
payments, they will remove the default status from your credit report and replace it with a new trade line that shows your
loans are current and have been current to allow you to start
rebuilding your credit.

I asked, "so how much am I going to be required to pay?"
We did a financial interview of sorts and based on my income, I'm only required to pay $5 a month. Yes, you read
that correctly. Five dollars a month. After 20 years, whatever
portion of the debt has not been paid will be wiped away.

I'm not sure why he decided to open up and share with me
about his personal experience, but I was certainly appreciative
to be speaking with someone who knew exactly where I was
coming from. He shared that he had gone to medical school
for two years and paid for it entirely with student loans.
When he took out the loans, he never imagined that he
wouldn't be a doctor or be unable to pay the loans back. I'm

sure he never saw himself essentially working for a collection's agency either. He was currently setup on an income-based repayment plan for his loans as well.

After we got off the phone, I felt relieved. That was one more thing that turned out far better than I expected. If there was ever a scripture that I should have tattooed on my forehead as a constant reminder every time I look in the mirror, it's Matthew 6:34. "Therefore, do not worry about tomorrow for tomorrow will worry about itself. Each day has enough trouble of its own."

Once I got off the phone with the student loan company, I went outside to check my mail. There was the envelope from the bankruptcy court. As I walked from the mailbox up to my house, I said out loud, "No matter what this says, everything is going to be okay. I know that God is working on my behalf. Everything that happens is for my good."

When I opened it up, it gave little to no information. All it said was that the debts had been discharged but it didn't specify which. There was a list of common debts that won't be discharged, which includes student loans. I felt defeated. I questioned if filing bankruptcy was the right decision. The biggest reason I did it was because I was hoping to get some relief from my student loan debt.

I called my brother to let him know that I received the letter saying the bankruptcy had been completed. I was nervous to call him. I never really know how he's going to react. I explained I would have to call on the loan he had co-signed for to find out what's going on but that I was going to wait a week for them to get the paperwork and their systems be updated.

He told me the account had already been closed on his credit report, his score dropped 10 points but now he's recovered and his score is back up. He wanted me to wait to see if they notify me. I explained to him that I'm not worried about the other loans. I don't have the money to pay them so there's nothing I can do about it, but I had told him before I would continue to pay this loan so it wouldn't negatively impact him. I didn't want him upset with me.

He told me that everything was going to be okay. He wasn't upset and we would handle whatever came next.

Then I did the worst thing you can do, I Googled. I had read numerous times that student loans could be discharged if there was a serious financial hardship. I make roughly $25,000 a year and my student loan payments are more than my monthly income. I think that qualifies as a serious financial hardship.

I started reading things I never saw the first time when I was looking for more information when trying to decide whether to file or not. One site said you had to petition specifically for the student loans to be discharged. Another site said that they would immediately call the loans due in full. My heart started racing. Short of winning the lottery, there was nothing I could do to fix this.

As I sat there on my couch, with a dog on each side of me, I prayed. I told God that I was scared. I didn't want to be but I was. There's no point in trying to hide it. God already knows anyway. "Cast all your anxiety on him because he cares for you." 1 Peter 5:7.

Repeat after me. "I trust you Jesus."

Can you believe that the month of June isn't over yet? I wasn't kidding when I said it needed its own chapter.

In September of last year (2018), I received a call from my bank letting me know that there was suspicious activity. They told me that someone had pretended to be me, used my license, but that no changes had been made or new accounts opened. However, they wanted me to change my online banking login and password, as well as putting a security code on my account to prevent anyone from being able to access it or make any unauthorized changes. After speaking with my bank, I went to the Sheriff's office to file a report.

They asked me for proof of the activity and I told them that I didn't have it. I assumed the bank would contact the authorities based on the information that had been given to me. It seemed as though someone had gone into a physical branch. The officer was less than helpful, but I can't exactly blame him. It's not as though they can take people's word and that be sufficient. I tried to get physical proof of some sort from my bank but they said there was none.

I called the credit reporting agencies and put a freeze on my credit as a precaution, even though my credit score is so low that no one would be able to get approved for a line of credit using my information.

A month later, my other bank account was compromised. Someone bought themselves a plane ticket. I determined that one had to be the result of a card skimmer at the gas station because that was the only activity on that account in weeks.

A few months later, I get an email from the Department of Motor Vehicles letting me know that my online account had been accessed. If it wasn't me, I should call their hotline. It wasn't me, so I called. They told me that someone did access my account, which would mean they have my name, address, date of birth and social security number, but they did not order a new driver's license or make any changes so there was nothing more they could do to help.

Imagine my surprise when I go to check my mail looking for my paycheck, only to receive a letter from a bank informing me that I've been enrolled in overdraft protection. I don't bank at this financial institution. I've never step foot in their bank. I wasn't even sure if there were any local branches. I Googled the phone number listed on the letter to see if it was in fact the bank's phone number. It was.

My initial reaction was that it could have been a fraudulent letter with a fake phone number that's used to scare someone into calling and entering their personal information into the automated system, only to have that information be stolen. However, that wasn't the case. It was legitimate and there was a branch not far from my house. I decided to go in person to see what information, if any, I could gather about who opened the account.

When I spoke to the teller, she was shocked as she had never seen this happen before. They had my name, address, social security number, and driver's license number correct. The phone number and email address used were different than mine. They also had some details of my driver's license incorrect. There was no money in the account. Of course. It was actually in the negative because they ordered checks.

I ended up having to sit down with one of the bankers to call the fraud department to request the account be investigated and closed. I was probably at the bank for two hours trying to get this taken care of. While we were waiting for someone in the fraud department to answer the phone, we were chatting about why someone would open a checking account in someone else's name. Apparently, one of the common reasons is to deposit a bad check into the account and then immediately withdraw the funds. In this day of mobile deposits and ATM deposits, there can be a small delay in the time between the check being received by the bank and it being flagged by the system as fake.

Thankfully, there had been no debit card issued on the account and there was a freeze on it preventing any withdrawals. The individual managed to get the account opened but the bank's security measures caught the inaccuracies and flagged the account. That was one silver lining to all of this.

After I finished at the bank, I contacted the police to file a report. They sent an officer to my house to take my statement. When I opened the door, I immediately recognized him. It was the same officer who I spoke with back in September when I received a call from Chase about something similar happening. Unfortunately, at that time, there was no physical evidence of a crime to be able to file a report. The second silver lining of an account actually being opened was that now I had proof someone was using my information.

The officer remembered me and the situation. I often wonder if it's a positive or a negative when people who I've only met once still remember me almost a year later. I even had the booklet he gave me in September sitting on my counter with the details of the day I spoke with him. He probably thought I was crazy, but I wanted to keep a record of everything that's happened

After hours of dealing with the bank and the sheriff, I finally had a case number. Actual documentation and proof that someone stole my personal information and was trying to use it to commit fraud. Jokes on them though. They stole the identity of a girl who'd just gone through bankruptcy and couldn't get credit if her life depended on it.

I will say one thing though; the past year has given me a lot of life experience. If you're not planning on applying for credit, I would definitely suggest calling each of the three credit bureau agencies and put a freeze on your account. You can also prevent a checking account from being opened by putting a freeze on ChexSystems.com. You'll receive a letter from each agency with a pin number to use to lift the freeze when needed. Take steps to prevent identity theft instead of having to respond once it's happened.

I expected that to be the end of the excitement for the day, but I was wrong. I walked outside with my dogs only to find that my pool had lost four plus inches of water in a single day. I was in shock. That was too much water for a simple leak like I had experienced in the past. I walked around the perimeter of the pool to see if the ground was wet. It wasn't. I called my dad to see if he had any ideas. This is the first time I've ever had a pool. He wasn't sure. I decided to turn on the pump to see if I could tell where the water was leaking out. After a few seconds I heard the spitting of water. I started screaming "I found it. I found it."

There was a PVC pipe that came out of the ground for the pump. The elbow joint had popped off. I was so thankful that it was an easy fix. Although, my dad thought I might have to cut off the other side and replace the top fitting, but I was going to try to glue it back together first to see if that would do the trick. He told me to dry it off and then sand the inside of the elbow joint and the outside of the other pipe before putting the glue on. Thankfully, I had the PVC glue from when we replaced the pool pump. It was easy enough to fix it up. I decided to wait until the following day to test it to see if it would hold.

The next morning, I debated on whether to go to the beach or not. We haven't had a rain free weekend in quite some time and it was gorgeous out. I decided to turn the pool pump on first just to make sure the glue held before leaving. I didn't want to risk it running for hours while I was gone and possibly burning up the pump due to no water. I flip the switch and the pump won't turn on. It just hummed.

I stood there annoyed. Seriously, now this? It worked fine last night. Based on past experience, I assumed it was likely the capacitor that had blown. Why, I wasn't sure, but that was the most likely cause for the pump not starting. Thank God for Amazon! I ordered a new capacitor for $10 with free next day delivery. I decided that I was not going to allow this to upset me or scare me. I'd replace the capacitor and go from there.

The next day, the capacitor arrived. I hooked it up and turned on the switch and the pump immediately turned on. Thank you, Jesus! I left it running to see if the glue was going to be sufficient to hold the PVC pipes together. After two hours, everything was still working perfectly. Although it was certainly unexpected and not how I wanted to spend my Friday and Saturday, I was beyond thankful that I was able to easily fix each problem I was faced with.

I used to joke that my dad taught me how to do things like mowing the yard just so that he wouldn't have to do them. Now, I'm thankful he taught me how to troubleshoot and fix things. The greatest blessing in the world, when you're a single woman who owns a home, is being able to repair things on your own without having to pay someone else to do every little thing for you.

We're still not out of the month of June!

On the 23rd, I checked my mail and there were four envelopes from Navient, who is the servicer for four of my student loans, one of which is the loan my brother co-signed on. The first letter I opened was to let me know that my student loans had not been discharged and would require repayment. My stomach may have dropped a little bit feeling somewhat defeated. The second letter was a reminder that the two federal loans that had been in an income-based repayment program were up for renewal and if I failed to renew, what my monthly payment would be.

I immediately got on my computer and went to the website to submit the renewal. It was re-approved. One crisis down. The other two letters were regarding the private loans. They were going back into repayment. Previously, I was paying $425 a month towards those loans. There was no way I was going to be able to swing that right now. I went online to see what the payment was and it showed that the loans were currently in a forbearance that would end July 9th.

On July 8th, I called to see what payment options could be made in hopes that post bankruptcy, perhaps they offered some type of program to help stay on track. The representative couldn't assist because the account was still reflecting the forbearance. He suggested I call back the following week once their system had updated.

Several days later my brother sends me a text message saying that the loan is back on his credit report. I was somewhat upset. My hope had been that at least maybe the loan wouldn't go back on his credit report. I told him that the student loans had not been discharged and I would still continue to have to pay them. I knew I would have to continue to pay that specific loan regardless, even if it had been discharged through bankruptcy for me, since the loan had a co-signer on it.

For now, all I can do is wait and see what happens. I know that no matter what, God is working it all out for my good. Would I have preferred to have all my private loans discharged through the bankruptcy? Of course, but obviously that wasn't part of God's plan. There's something else coming that will make this seem insignificant. I truly believe that.

On a positive note, we made it to the end of June. Longest. Month. Ever.

Chapter Eleven

We must have the faith that things will work out somehow, that God will make a way for us when there seems no way.
– Martin Luther King, Jr.

Hello July!

With the bankruptcy being completed, I find myself checking my mail less frequently. I probably check it once a week now. I had just come home from the gym and the trash had been picked up so I decided to check the mail before bringing the trash cans back up to the house. I was sorting through it as I walked back up to the house and saw that there was something from the bankruptcy trustee, my homeowner's insurance company, and my student loan company. I could feel my anxiety start to increase.

I was trying to get into my house when my neighbor called my name. I looked up and he was walking across his yard to come talk to me. I was trying to be polite even though I really wanted to get inside to see what all this mail was. My neighbor is such a nice guy. He wanted to make sure that I knew his family reunion was the coming weekend. He always wants to make sure I know that if anyone parks on my grass or blocks my driveway, to come over and let him know. It's really consid-erate of him, and I greatly appreciate the way he looks out for me on a regular basis.

I kept slowly backing away from him hoping he would realize that I needed to go without being rude. I really wanted to know what the letter from the bankruptcy trustee said. Finally, he started to wrap up the conversation and I went inside. Which one should I open first?

I decided to open the mail from the bankruptcy trustee first. The heading that it was the trustee's final report. I was hoping it would show me what had been discharged and what had not been, but it wasn't that kind of report. Do you remember the $1518 that I had to pay the trustee in order to keep my car? The report was to show how those funds were allocated amongst my creditors.

There was a claim from the IRS listed that I didn't understand. It was for roughly $3700. Was that what the IRS estimated I owed for 2018? When I filed my extension, $2200 was what I estimated that I would owe. Next to it, it showed an applied amount of roughly $1100.

The next line, it showed the trustee's fees that totaled approximately $400. To the right, it showed $400 had been applied. No other creditors had received any portion of the $1518.

Does that mean that $1100 had been applied towards my 2018 taxes? I decided to email the trustee and ask. I received a response back within ten minutes. She said, "Here's the claim from the IRS. That's exactly what it looks like!" I learned through our previous interactions that she has to be very tight lipped. Typically, the response is, "I cannot be your lawyer." The trustee is a neutral party that's assigned by the court to examine your paperwork for accuracy and to sell off any assets to pay creditors that you're not by law allowed to retain. They cannot offer any legal advice.

I knew from her response that she was confirming that the IRS had filed a claim against me for the estimated amount of taxes that would be due for 2018, and she applied all the remaining funds towards that claim. Here's the crazy thing. On several occasions, when thinking about how I had to come up with money to pay my taxes for 2018, I often thought how it would have been nice to have those stocks to sell to apply towards it. Only to have that happen anyway. The stock sale benefited me in the bankruptcy and then again with my taxes.

Only God could orchestrate the same money being used to benefit two debts. But wait, it gets better.

The next envelope I opened was from the company that I have my homeowner's insurance through. My insurance is escrowed with my mortgage payment. You may recall I mentioned that this past February I received a check from my mortgage company in the amount of $550 for an escrow overage. I was nervous that the letter was going to say that there was a shortage or my premium was going up, which would cause my monthly mortgage payment to increase.

As I opened the envelope, I could tell it was a single page document. As I went to turn it over, I saw that it was actually a check. Yes, another check. This one in the amount of $78 for over payment. What are the odds? I'm guessing not very likely.

I hope I don't lose you here, but I think this is worth mentioning. I've seen people on social media talk about manifesting dreams. It never really made sense to me. I am part of a 21-day challenge group on Facebook to work through the book Unstoppable Influence by Natasha Hazlett. I decided to pose the question to the group asking for practical information on how people do this.

I took their advice and started doing it. I visualize the life I want. I speak the things that I want out loud for God and the universe to hear. I've been praying for God's favor and abundance. As part of my daily manifesting, I say, "Thank you God for your financial abundance. I receive money from unlikely sources all the time." When you're in a hard place and you can't tell where you're going to get the money that you need, it can be difficult to state with specificity when manifesting things into existence. Instead, I decided to focus on receiving money from unlikely sources because I can't honestly fathom where the money could come from.

That's the thing about serving an all-powerful God. A God who can do the imaginable. I know that anything is possible. I'm not trying to tell God how to be God. I'm focusing more on releasing control and trusting God. I know that God will fulfill His promises to me.

As I've been writing this, I've also been reading The Circle Maker. It's helped me to realize that God wants me to pray big prayers. There's nothing wrong with having big dreams, dreams that so far exceed what you think you're capable of, because God is capable of all things. There is nothing too big for our God.

I needed that reminder as I was faced with the third letter, from my student loan company. This was the dreaded letter. I knew that I was going to have to start paying again but I didn't know when or how much the payment would be. When I opened it, it was a statement showing that I had a payment of $451 due on August 4th.

I won't lie and say that I immediately thought, "Hey, no big deal, I have an all-powerful God." Definitely not my first thought. It was more something like, "there's no way I'm going to be able to come up with this payment every month. I struggle to make ends meet now."

I decided to call customer service again to see if there was anything they could do to help me. The original representative told me the only thing they could do would be to bring down the monthly amount to $375. I explained that I was hoping for more like $200, which would still be hard but I would find a way to make it work. She told me they had nothing else they could offer me, but that I could speak with the collections department to see if they could help. However, since my loan was not past due, they might not be able to assist.

I had her transfer me to the collections department and I explained to the representative that I had just completed my bankruptcy so there was literally no money left to be able to make this payment. Again, she told me they could reduce it to $375 and I explained that I wouldn't be able to make the payment. She looked for any other offers and said they could do a six-month, interest only, payment program for me that would bring the payment down to $262 a month. The catch, I had to have it auto drafted every month.

When you're playing as closely with money as I am, auto draft is nothing but anxiety. I currently have my car insurance on auto draft and it's supposed to come out on the 17th but it's literally never the same day of the month. Then, some months, I won't get my paycheck in time to have the funds in the account. Once, the insurance was canceled for non-payment because I didn't get my paycheck until 3 days after they tried to withdraw the funds.

Some of you are probably laughing because you know exactly what I'm talking about. You've been there. You've lived through something similar. It's awful. The car insurance is the only bill that gets paid "on time" based on when they withdraw it. Everything else can be anywhere from a week to three weeks late every month. It just depends on what date pay day falls on.

Even though I wasn't thrilled about the auto draft, I was thankful that for at least six months, I had a lower payment until I could try to figure out a way to increase my income. Right now, my dad is up north. He spends his winters in Florida and his summers up in New Jersey. He's really embracing that retirement lifestyle. While he's out of town, he pays me $100 a month to mow his yard for him. He figures, he would have to pay someone else to do it, might as well pay me.

Last summer, I sort of dreaded it. While I liked having the extra $100, the actual mowing of the yard seemed to be a huge pain. This summer, I've gotten a little better with my routine. I've been getting up at 6:15am to run each morning, so I go directly to my dad's house when I'm done every Friday and mow his yard. So far, I've been able to get home and shower before the emails start coming in for work.

My dad also sends me $100 every month for his portion of the car insurance, since we have a family plan. I setup the auto draft for the student loans to come out of the joint bank account I have with my dad. He typically deposits the $200 around the 1st of each month. I figured, this way, I'll only have to worry about depositing $62 into that account by the 4th when the student loans are auto withdrawn. It's not a perfect solution, since I typically rely on that extra $100-$200 for groceries, but it's something.

I haven't had very much luck finding good transcription jobs to be able to bring in extra money. The summer tends to be slower according to the forum all of us use to communicate with each other. This month has also been slower for the corporate housing business. We did seven new setups in June. I was really hoping for 10 in July, but so far, it's only been one.

I try to remind myself that I can't get discouraged when things start to go well and then seem to fall right back into the struggle again. This is how God is able to tell if I've really grown or not. Am I trusting him? Or do I immediately go back to the doom and gloom scenarios? I do think that I've gotten significantly better about checking my mindset and reactions to things. While I'm certainly far from perfect, I'm really pleased with my progress. I know that I'm growing, and that makes me incredibly happy.

Do you remember earlier I talked about a Facebook group I was a part of where we did 21-day challenges to help with personal growth and to help change our mindset? There's a challenge almost every month, although it's not always the same focus. Each challenge cost $47.

The woman behind it all, Natasha Hazlett, had shared that she was going to be making a big announcement on July 10th. She's always up to something so it definitely piqued my interest. She went live in our alumni group and shared that they had decided to start an Unstoppable for Life group, which would be $47 a month and as a member of that group you got access to all the challenges for free. There would also be additional monthly trainings in the Unstoppable for Life group.

I was already investing the money almost monthly for the challenges because I could see how they were positively benefiting my life, and the additional training topics she talked about were certainly something I didn't want to miss out on. I decided to go ahead and join even though it meant another monthly auto draft. I told myself I would have to stay up late or get up early to find transcription jobs to do to bring in the extra income to make sure I had the funds to cover it monthly.

I found one job to complete on Monday evening, which was graded on Tuesday. I received a perfect score, but it didn't raise my average very much. In order to maintain my account, I had to have a 4.5/5 average. In the very beginning, there were training transcription assignments they suggest that you do. One of them was really hard but I thought it was important for me to still try to do it. I scored a 3. That one score was impossible to try to overcome. Thankfully, in 120 days it would fall off, so I was about 25 days away from my score being almost perfect.

The next day I received another email about a grade. I hadn't done any transcription jobs so I wasn't sure what had been graded. I opened it to read the details and the very first transcription job I had done was re-graded. The score dropped me below a 4.5 average. They said you could appeal, so I tried.

I never received a response to my appeal. They sent me an email saying that my account had been closed due to my score dropping below 4.5. And just like that I found myself distraught and upset. Even though it was only an extra $150-$200 a month, it was the sense of knowing that if I needed money for gas or groceries, I'd be able to bring in some money quickly since they paid weekly.

The very next day Marisol, who had done my hair, sent me a text to check in on me. I told her how things were going and that I'd just lost the extra income from doing the transcription work. She tells me that she's been babysitting over the summer to bring in additional income since she works at a school and is off during the summer months. Her and her husband were going out of town for a week and the woman she babysits for needed someone for one or two days, would I be interested.

Okay, so let's just go ahead and put this out there. I'm not the best with kids. Despite my very strong desire to be a parent, I have a very low tolerance for dealing with other people's kids. I explained my hesitations to her and she assured me that I could handle it. It was two boys who were old enough to take care of themselves, but one of them had Down syndrome.

I almost immediately said no. I did not feel at all equipped to be able to adequately supervise or assist with a special needs child. She assured me that it wouldn't be hard and asked me to come by the next morning to meet the boys and their mom. She would show me their routine so I would be comfortable. I agreed although I was still feeling extremely apprehensive about it.

This is one of those moments where I have this internal conversation with myself about how I'm standing in the way of a blessing for myself, being a blessing to someone else, and allowing someone else to be a blessing to me. Why? Fear. Fear of the unknown. Fear of not being capable. Fear of something going wrong. Fear of something happening. Just straight fear.

The next morning, I went over and met the boys and their mom. The mom and her son with Down syndrome were sitting at the kitchen counter eating breakfast. Marisol introduced us and we all said our hellos. As Marisol is talking, the little boy starts blowing me kisses. It was the sweetest, most unexpected response. His mom was quite surprised as well.

Maybe he could tell I was nervous. I'm not sure, but it certainly put me more at ease. The following Monday I showed up to babysit. It was expected to be about 4 hours. I had a lot of anxiety. I knew that I was supposed to cook them breakfast, which was probably my greatest source of anxiety. For one, I don't really cook but secondly, I was concerned about not cooking it correctly and the boys not wanting to eat because it wasn't what they were used to.

I walked inside and the little boy with down syndrome came running up to me and gave me a hug. His mom commented on how he doesn't usually take to people so quickly. To my delight she had already made them breakfast too. A huge sigh of relief for me. The only thing left to do was for him to put on his swim trunks and sunscreen to get in the pool. His morning routine was spending about 3 hours playing in the pool. His brother came out and played too for some of it.

The skies started to get dark so we had to go inside earlier than I'm sure he would have preferred. His brother was such an amazing help getting whatever I needed and I made sure to let his mom know when she got home. She was really happy to hear they had both been so great. As I was leaving, she sent me $40 via PayPal for watching them for roughly 3 hours.

Had I let my fear stop me, I would have never experienced the sweet, loving and really just beautiful moments with this little boy with Down syndrome. His mom would have had to miss an important meeting at work and probably more importantly, had to go grocery shopping with the kids as opposed to going alone after her meeting. I would have prevented myself from receiving $40, and I would have prevented my friend Marisol from having the joy of knowing she helped me during my time of need.

August 2019

I am a firm believer in personal development. I think self-help books can be really impactful. I truly believe that participating in something as simple as a 21-day challenge can truly change your life – IF – if you are willing to put in the work not just during the challenge or while reading the book, but in the days, weeks and months that follow.

You can read all the books in the world but if you don't take the steps required to put into action the things that you've learned, you're not going to make any progress. I shared earlier that I've been reading The Circle Maker. I have been praying bigger, bolder prayers. I've been setting bigger goals. I felt that I needed to do more. I decided going into the month of August that I was going to fast every Monday for a year.

I was asking God for a new stream of income. I decided I needed to do more than just pray. In The Circle Maker, Mark

Batterson shared, "Fasting has a way of fast-tracking our prayers. Because fasting is harder than praying, fasting is a form of praying hard. In my experience, it is the shortest distance to a breakthrough." (Batterson, 2011) He goes on to say that "Fasting gives you more power to pray because it's an exercise in willpower."

I needed a breakthrough. I wasn't asking for a winning lottery ticket. I wasn't asking for all my problems and struggles to go away. More than anything, I just didn't want to have to worry that my mortgage was going to get paid every month. As I'm writing this, it's currently one month past due and I don't know how I am going to be able to get caught up short of a miracle.

I had a bit of an emotional breakdown when I was on the phone with my brother. I greatly dislike crying in front of people, especially those who tend to think you're so strong. I was going through a really hard time. Life felt overwhelming. Despite knowing that what I see every day on social media is not an accurate representation of people's lives, there are still times where I find myself in the comparison trap.

Okay, so maybe my mortgage payment wasn't the only thing that I was asking God for. At the end of April, I ended an almost three year long relationship. When I met him, I made it very clear that church and God were huge parts of my life. I had no interest in being with someone who didn't have my same beliefs. Without getting into too much of the story, his mom was a minister at one of my favorite pastor's church. He knew the bible better than I did, which wasn't necessarily challenging but it did make me happy.

Perhaps it was my longing desire to find someone to build a life with that I was convinced the only reason our paths crossed was because of God. He didn't live in Florida. I just happened to be going to the city he lived in for an event, which is when we met. Because I wanted so badly to believe he was sent from God, I ignored the red flags early on that could have saved me from a lot of hurt.

I try to always learn from experiences so that I can do better the next time. As I was reading the Circle Maker, Batterson shared a story about how his grandfather would pray over him every night. "And even though he died when I was six, his prayers did not. Our prayers never die." (Batterson, The Circle Maker, 2011) As I read those words, tears started running down my face. I can remember when I was younger, my mom used to pray for my future husband.

I bought a book once that focused on prayers for your future spouse but I don't know that I got through even half of it. It's never been something I've been diligent with or even remotely focused on. But now, after having gone through everything I went through over the last 32 months, I knew I needed to put God at the center of my romantic life as well.

As I continued trying to put words into action, I decided to see if any of my single friends would be interested in doing a 40-day prayer circle with me. This too was discussed in The Circle Maker and where I saw the idea to do it. To my surprise, there were several women who immediately said yes. On the day we started, there were 11 of us total.

By linking up together with other single women, I was able to not only activate my faith and but I also helped other women to activate theirs. There is power in linking arms with like-minded people. It's not just true with business. Being surrounded by women who are there to listen when you need it, who will speak the word of God over you, and have empathy for what you're going through because they are either currently experiencing the same or have experienced those same feelings as well.

I wanted to share this with you to reiterate the value of having people in your life that you can talk to and share your struggles with. Our lives are full of many different types of struggles, not just financial ones. You need people you can do life with. All aspects of your life with. We live in a society where people project the highlights of their life while hiding the struggles. This has created a culture where people think that if they're struggling, they must be doing something wrong.

If you're struggling, you're doing something right friends! I can't tell you the number of times I've thought to myself how much easier my life was when I was living for myself. It was easier because I wasn't a threat to the devil. The number of spiritual attacks I've experienced since I started writing this book have been many. I shared that with you earlier. Writing this has been hard on so many levels, but I'm not stopping. I don't care how long it takes me to finish this book. I will finish it and it will impact the lives of those whose hands it is meant to reach.

Never be ashamed of your struggle. Never be afraid to share your struggle. Your struggle may be the key to someone else's freedom.

September 2019

One of the biggest reasons I absolutely love my pastor is his willingness to be blunt with us. He doesn't sugar coat topics. He's not trying to win a popularity contest. He wants us to live our best life with Christ at the center.

It's easy for us to say we're praying about something and we're going to let go and let God. The problem with that is we're not taking responsibility for the part we play in making things happen in our lives. Mark Batterson said it best, "pray like it depends on God and work like it depends on you."

Life has been calm. Nothing crazy happening, which is how I prefer it most days. Out of the blue, my dad sends me an email he received from the attorney's office for a deposition. I, on the other hand, had not received anything. Of course, I immediately was nervous wondering why they would only want to speak with my dad.

My mind started racing. I don't know if you're like me but my mind can come up with a hundred different scenarios in a matter of minutes that will put me into a complete state of panic. My first thought was that they were going to force my dad to sell his motorcycles to pay down some of the debt.

My heart sank. The absolute last thing I ever wanted was for my dad to lose what he's worked so hard for because of me. That night, before bed, I got on my knees and I prayed through my tears. I asked God for a financial miracle. I did not want my dad to lose anything. This was my responsibility. I knew I couldn't fix it on my own but I knew that God had the power to.

I cried. I begged. I pleaded. My heart hurt.

I went to YouTube and started playing "I Raise A Hallelujah" on my phone. I laid in bed, singing along, as the tears rolled down my face. Eventually, I fell asleep emotionally exhausted.

The next morning as I got out of bed, I continued to sing "I raise a hallelujah, in the presence of my enemies. I raise a hallelujah, louder than the unbelief. I raise a hallelujah, my weapon is a melody. I raise a hallelujah, heaven comes to fight for me." I didn't know what else to do. I didn't know what else to say to God, so I sang.

Around noon I received an email asking to schedule a phone interview for one of the jobs that I had applied for. It was one that I really wanted and would put me at or close to earning six figures a year. I was shocked. Did that really just happen? Is this my answered prayer?

They wanted to do a phone interview the following day. I spent the entire rest of my day reading everything I could on their leadership principals and the mission of the company. I wanted to be as prepared as possible. I found common questions they ask and tried to prepare my answers ahead of time.

I continued to praise and worship throughout the day. I prayed throughout the day. My heart was so full with anticipation.

The following day, interview day, I woke up excited by the possibilities. I laid in bed the night before thinking about how different my life would be if I was making three times the amount of money I am now.

My heart was racing as I watched the minutes turn by leading up to the call. I knew that if this was for me, nothing could stand in the way of it.

The call had been scheduled for 45 minutes, but she said it wouldn't last more than 15. It was just a quick call to get to know me better and explain about the position.

The conversation was easy. We were in agreement on topics discussed. She said she was happy to hear some of my responses. She went into so much detail about the job, talking about it as if it was already mine. Then she would catch herself and say, if you're selected of course. At the end, she told me she was going to pass me back to the recruiter to schedule a face to face interview with another manager and someone from Human Resources.

I got off the phone elated. I was so happy with how well the call went, how easy the conversation flowed, and how it seemed like the interviewer, who would be my boss, could already see me in the role. Again, I kept praising and worshiping. Thanking God for the opportunity. I was supposed to hear back within 48 hours.

164 · MS RACHEL MARIE

I decided to wait until Tuesday to follow up. I received a response back on Thursday that they had decided not to
proceed further with the interview process. I was devastated.

But why God? How did this happen? I don't understand how
it could go from being such a positive experience, saying that
she wanted me to do more interviews, to we've decided not
to proceed.

I am an analytical person. I pick apart sentences. I hone in on
fluctuations in pitch and tone. I literally dissected every second of the interview trying to determine where it shifted.
What happened to make her decide not to proceed? I went
over the interview in my head a hundred times. I couldn't
understand where I went wrong.

How could something that seemed timed so perfectly from
God end up like this? Was it just to get my hopes up for
nothing? My heart hurt. I had shared with two different prayer circles about what had happened, from applying and my
prayer of desperation to getting the interview. Everyone responded the same – "It's already yours."

Why? Why God? I don't understand why!

I gave myself time to calm down and breath before apologizing to God for my lack of trust. I was reminded in that
moment that it's easy to trust God when things are going
your way, but the true trusting happens when things are not
going your way. I sat there and asked myself, *do you believe that
God has a plan for your life? Do you believe that God is faithful? Do
you believe that God's word is true? Do you believe that God's promises
will come to pass in your life? If you truly believe the answer to these
questions is yes, you cannot allow the enemy even 5 minutes to plant
seeds of doubt in your mind.*

Sometimes I have to speak hard truths to myself in order to
prevent the enemy from winning that battle. Would it have

been a victory for God if I was able to then go back and share with my prayer circles that I got the job? Of course. But what greater testimony is it to be able to say I know that God has something better in store for me, and this is God's way of protecting me from something that was not for me and keeping me available for what is. How you handle those moments of disappointment is where you have the greatest opportunity to be a witness.

I brushed myself off and I got back on my computer to start looking for more jobs to apply for. I came across this website that was designed to help women find jobs. They also gave reviews on a variety of different employers. Out of curiosity, I looked up the employer who I had the interview with to see what people were saying. Quite frankly, I was shocked. There wasn't much good said regarding the way women were treated or their ability to advance their careers.

That reaffirmed for me that despite seeming perfect to me at the time, God always knows more than we know and everything always works out for our highest good.

November 2019

The next blessing is one I am a little scared to share about. I don't know if I can get in trouble for this or not, but it was a blessing for me so here we go.

Remember when I shared how in March, I was advised by the bankruptcy trustee that I had to pay $1518 in order to be able to keep my car? Then in July I received a notice from the trustee listing out how that money had been distributed to my creditors with $1100 going to the IRS to be applied towards my 2018 taxes, which had not yet been filed.

The only rationale I can come up with for why the IRS estimated my 2018 taxes to be over $3000 was due to the expected annual income listed when determining my health care subsidy. I believe my insurance agent put down $22,000 even though I explained that it would definitely not be that much and wanted her to use the lowest possible amount allowed to still qualify. Apparently, that never happened. When it got to the point that I could no longer afford the $136 monthly payment for health insurance, I reached out to the company I had gone through to request an income change. They lowered my income down to $13999, which is the lowest amount allowed to still receive a subsidy. That reduced my monthly payment to $67. During the conversations to reduce my income, I learned that I was not required to meet a minimum income during 2018 but only for 2019, since that is the year I'm receiving the subsidy.

I waited until the absolute last minute to do my 2018 taxes. We're talking I filed them the day before the cut off. I ended up owing $583. I submitted my return. On November 7th, I receive a check in the mail from the IRS for $469.50 - the balance from the $1100 paid by the trustee towards my 2018 taxes and the fine for not paying by April 15, 2019.

Thanks to that money, I was able to pay my mortgage in November. It's been a rough couple of months. Business has been much slower than it was the year prior. To be honest, I never expected it would be so hard to find a job in corporate America. I pray every night that God will provide a financial miracle, another stream of income, etc. It's hard to be in a season of waiting, but I do know without a shadow of a doubt that there's something incredible ahead.

Mid-month my eGroup had Friendsgiving. To open, we all went around the table to share at least one thing that we were grateful for that has happened this past year. I'll recap with you what I shared with the group.

> In our society today, we often hear the quote "Comparison is the thief of all joy" and it can be. We often compare our waist size, bust size, house size, family

size, etc. We tend to focus on the things that others have that we want but don't yet have. However, I'm in a season where the ability to compare is what brings me joy. Had I not experienced the bad, I would not be able to fully appreciate the good. In fact, I may have missed the good all together or dismissed it. So, the thing I'm most grateful for this year is a shift in perspective.

We were fortunate to have Jenn, our campus pastor's wife, visiting our eGroup that night. I adore her. She has a true heart for people. I really don't know how she does it. She expressed how she has watched me grow over the last four years and what I had shared demonstrates true spiritual growth.

Then our eGroup leader, LaShaundra, said she wanted to piggy back on that and share how proud she is that despite everything I have been going through during this season, I was still obedient and followed the call God laid on my heart to start a prayer circle that blessed others. I followed the call when no one would have known any different had I not. I didn't allow my struggles or hardships to stop me from saying yes to God's call.

In that moment, as she was speaking about how I could have ignored the calling placed on my heart, I realized that she wasn't really speaking about the prayer circle. God was using her to speak to me about this very book. It hasn't been the easiest to write and I certainly have a long list of reasons why I don't want to publish it.

I could set it aside. I could wait years to write the conclusion expecting that I would have something profound to share like a six figure a year job. But the reality is, that's me waiting on a winning lottery ticket before I'm willing to share God's faithfulness in the small things, which is the entire point of this book.

So I sit here and push forward. I continue to write knowing that the reason I'm doing this has little to do with me and everything to do with God.

December 2019

This time of year is always hard for me emotionally. I can remember when I was growing up how exciting the holidays were. I absolutely loved the traditions we had. Thanksgiving was probably my favorite because I've always been a lover of food. It was the only time when we would eat turkey, stuffing or pumpkin pie. The day after Thanksgiving we would always put up the Christmas tree. We had an artificial tree but it was still just as fun.

The weeks leading up to Christmas were always filled with making Christmas cookies and decorating them. I remember all the neighborhood kids would come over one Saturday to decorate cookies. We had so much fun. I loved watching as more and more gifts would show up under the tree. I was never that kid who tried to find the gifts beforehand. I didn't shake the boxes to try and guess. I lived for the excitement of Christmas morning.

In the years following my mom's death, we barely celebrated holidays. I tried for a couple years to make Thanksgiving dinner with my brother but we never put up a tree. We didn't really give gifts anymore. It was as if my mom was the glue that held everything together, the center which everything revolved around.

Now, at the age of 39, it's become a time of year when I think more about how I don't have a husband and family to continue those traditions with. As I shared before, with the prevalence of social media, it's so easy to fall into the comparison trap. I find this time of year I'm more likely to fall for the lies the devil loves to fill my head with. Then add the feelings of inadequacy that are bubbling up after having applied for 40 plus jobs and not getting any interviews. Plus, the financial stressors.

It's been very hard to remain focused on trusting that God has a plan and a purpose for my life. It's getting harder to have faith that the best is yet to come. I'm struggling to hold onto hope.

It was a Friday evening, I was driving to eGroup with my friend Terry. We were talking about how work was and my job hunt. I jokingly commented maybe I should get a job at Hooters and use what God gave me to make some money. I was kidding around. I'm self-aware enough to know that being a server is not something I could excel at.

We arrive at eGroup and LaShaundra starts by opening us up in prayer. She asked if there were any prayer requests. I didn't say anything. She looks at me and says, I can see the stress all over your face. Ugh, I thought to myself, I never was any good at controlling my face.

She starts praying, addressing the prayer requests for those who have asked, and she walks around the table and stands next to me, puts her arm around me and starts praying that I would find a job that would allow me to pay my bills each month and then some. As she continued, her praying turned into prophesying. I sat there with tears running down my face as she spoke over me. Telling me not to compromise myself for money. God had a plan in place and I needed to wait on Him. The Holy Spirit spoke through her to me for a good 10 minutes. I had tears and snot running down my face.

No one sitting around that table knew exactly what I'd been thinking about for the days leading up to our gathering. No one knew the ways I was thinking about how I could make some easy money. No one knew how active the devil was in my thoughts. No one knew.

When she finished, I looked at Terry and said, "I was only kidding about getting a job at Hooters." I said it to lighten the mood, but what I was really feeling was such a huge conviction that I had actually considered not only compromising myself and my body, but my relationship with God – for money.

When I was feeling hopeless, abandoned and forgotten by God, he used someone I greatly admire and adore to breath life back into me. It was through her that God made it clear He had not forgotten or abandoned me. Friends, this is why it's so important to surround yourself with people who can speak not only words of encouragement over your life but the word of God as well.

As humans, we have a tendency to be apprehensive and skeptical. If someone you barely know or someone you don't really care for tried to give you advice, you probably wouldn't take it to heart. At least, I know I wouldn't. There's no doubt in my mind that God used this specific person to speak to me. He knew that it had to be someone I had the utmost respect for and admired. Truly, He could not have picked a better person to speak through.

I believe wholeheartedly that God has used very specific people at different times to speak to me regarding my circumstances at those specific moments. We don't always know who and what we need, but God certainly does.

Two weeks later, while enjoying a seafood boil with my eGroup sisters, I received a notification from PayPal that I had a payment from my sister-in-law. In addition to my base pay, she also gave me $1000 for Christmas. I was so beyond shocked and grateful. I would be able to use those funds to get caught up on my mortgage.

God shows up when you least expect it, and, sometimes, He even uses those you least expect grant a blessing. Keep your heart open to receive that which God has prepared for you. You're not forgotten. You haven't been abandoned. Your prayers never die.

Conclusion

If you're struggling today, remember that life is worth living and believe
that the best is yet to come. Remember that you are loved, you matter,
and never forget that there is always hope.
— Germany Kent

2019 certainly proved to be a challenging year for me. While I
expected it to end vastly different than it did, I am thankful
for all that God has done for me and through me over these
last 365 days. My word for 2019 was freedom and I received
so much of it this past year.

I have continuously delayed writing this final chapter because
I felt as though I couldn't finish it without having some
amazing and profound miracle that changed the trajectory of
my life. What good would a book about God's promises and
faithfulness be if it didn't end with rainbows and butterflies?
People want to know if they are obedient, they're going to
receive all of God's promises.

Every good story has a victorious ending, right? The guy gets
the girl. The cop catches the bad guy. The soldier saves the
country. Or in my case, the girl lands an amazing job.

I left this sitting for months. Hoping that something huge
and transformational would happen, that I would be able to
use as my conclusion to prove to people if you stay faithful in
the little things, God will be faithful in the big things.

Here's the thing though. I have said from the beginning that
the whole reason I decided to start writing this book was to
help others to see the way God works in the tiny details of

our lives. It's not about big grandiose gestures. It's not about a winning lotto ticket. It's about the spiritual growth that takes place when you fully trust God during your seasons of struggle.

If we look at the bible, there are many stories where God's promise to do exceedingly and abundantly more than we could ask or imagine came to pass. We read it and we see BIG blessings. Take Job for example, he lost everything but then God gave him even more in return. We see the sacrifice followed by a big blessing. What we don't tend to focus on is the amount of time between the two events.

God's timing is not our timing. We want to make one small sacrifice and receive a big blessing. We are willing to trust for a few months, but then we need God to show up big in our lives. We don't feel as though we've been blessed by God if we are still experiencing hardships and struggles.

We expect God's blessing to come in the form of no more hardships and no more struggles. Friends, please understand that God is never going to create a world in which He is no longer needed. That is not the way God works. There will be a list, much like the one you've just read, where God will bless you in the little things, in the mundane, in the ordinary walk of YOUR life. God is blessing you always.

I could wait 10, 20, even 40 years to publish this book so that I could have a better ending. One that ends in financial success. I could, but then the entire premise behind why God laid it on my heart to write this book would be lost. I recently shared this on Facebook and I think it's exactly the big profound ending this book was supposed to have –

> *The greatest things that have happened in my life no one knows about, they aren't tangible, they can't be photographed to post on social media, they don't come with a huge pay raise or a tiny waist...*

The greatest things that have happened in my life happened to me, for me, to become the best me... they came in the form of hope, peace, and gratitude to name a few.

That is my happy ending. It's celebrating that now when I feel overwhelmed, I don't fall back into old self sabotaging behaviors. It's celebrating that now I turn to God first and friends second. It's celebrating that I have experienced God in an intimate way. It's celebrating that I'm not the same person I was a year ago.

What should you be celebrating friends?

We have to be willing to praise God in the middle. We have to celebrate God's faithfulness in the midst of the chaos. We have to be willing to follow the call God places on our heart even when we feel unqualified.

I hope you never wait to share your story of the goodness of God until you think it fits the standards of what the world would consider a miracle. Most miracles aren't big and grandiose. The world needs to know about all the small miracles so they can see God working in their life as much as he's working in yours and mine.

Go.

Share.

Share now.

The "But God" Bonus Chapter

I was all set to publish. I met with my friend at the beach to do a little photo shoot to create my cover photo. Everything was moving forward with an expected date to publish.

But then God stepped in.

In order to fully explain what's happened in the last couple weeks, I have to start from the beginning of the year. I had continued to apply for jobs that I found online but there hadn't been any interviews scheduled.

In December of 2019, a former employee and friend reached out to me to let me know that the company she was working for had recently let go several people in management. They were looking to change the culture of the company and now might be the best chance I'd have of coming in at a leadership level.

This particular company is notorious for hiring from within. I had applied several times before. They had put me through multiple interviews only to not get the job. One department was because executive leadership decided due to funding, they couldn't hire any additional staffing. Another time it was because they decided to go with an internal candidate.

Part of me had settled with the idea that I was simply not meant to work there and wasn't going to apply again. Another part of me knew that they were probably the only way for me to get back to making decent money in this town. I decided to give it another chance.

Within days of submitting my application, I received an email about a phone interview. I had been through this twice so I knew how it would go. Or at least I thought I did.

When the time for the interview had come, I waited for the call. My phone rings. I answer and the person asks for someone else. The same number calls back almost ten minutes later and asks for me. He explains that the system had messed up and he got confused about who

178 · MS RACHEL MARIE

the interview was with. I tried to make light of it joking about the full moon effecting even technology.

The interviewer had no personality. He literally ran down the list of questions that are asked on the website when you apply. I thought it was really strange and quite frankly, a waste of time. I asked some questions about the position and he didn't even acknowledge or respond to them. Once we finished that, he asked me three other questions. I confirmed while I was talking that I wasn't speaking too quickly as the interviewer said nothing to acknowledge he was even listening.

I got off the phone thinking *could that have gone any worse*? I should have known not to think that. Almost 30 minutes later, I get a call from that same number. I answered and it's the same interviewer. He tells me that the computer didn't save any of my responses but he could remember all of my answers except for one.

I'm thankful that this transpired on the phone so he couldn't see my face. Based on how the interview went, I didn't have a whole lot of confidence in his ability to remember my answers. But honestly, what could I do? If I challenged him, I ran the risk of bruising his ego and him not passing me along to the hiring manager. I had to just accept it and do my best to extend grace while going over my answer for a second time.

I reached out to my friend who had suggested the job to tell her how it went. She encouraged me to remain positive.

Over a month had gone by and nothing. My friend said that they still hadn't filled the position so she would reach out to the hiring manager, whom she knew, to put in a good word. It wasn't until February when I received an email to schedule two more interviews. One would be with the hiring managers and the other would be with the other supervisors who would be my peers.

I was excited. I was hopeful. I was … desperate. I really needed to find a new job. There's a reason why people always say you shouldn't work for family. It was starting to become unhealthy for me.

I spent so much time leading up to the interviews praying, asking God to give me the right words, to help me to retrieve appropriate memories to answer the questions well. I knew that this company liked to do situational questions such as "Tell me a time when …" I didn't want to sit there for any length of time with an awkward silence as I was trying to recollect a time to answer their question.

As I drove to the interview location, I had praise and worship music playing. I drove, I sang and I prayed. I had poured my heart out to God. He knew exactly where I was, how I was feeling, and what I wanted.

The interviews went really well. The questions were easy to answer. There were no awkward silences. The energy was good. There was a lot of agreement with how I handled various situations. They indicated during the interview that they should have a determination by the end of the week. I felt really good about it when I left.

The end of the week came, and I heard nothing. Another week went by and still no word. I reached out to my friend to see if she knew anything and she said that she'd see what she could find out.

Apparently, they were still conducting interviews. I kept trying to tell myself what was meant for me no man could stand in the way of. But I was losing faith.

Two and a half weeks later, I received a phone call from their human resources department asking if I was still interested in the position. I excitingly told him I absolutely was.

He informed me that they were going to do another round of interviews but this time it would be with the director and the vice president. This would be my fourth interview for this position.

Initially, I was told I would hear back in a day or so to schedule the interview. After a week, I decided to reach out to the gentleman that had called to see if there was an update. He responded quickly to let me know that there had been a delay but they were still going to schedule the interviews.

In an interesting twist of fate, there were now two positions available with three candidates going through another round of interviews. While I didn't want to get my hopes up, I was so excited. I had a one in three chance of getting the position.

It took almost two weeks to schedule, and then the interview wasn't for another two weeks. The delays disappointed me. I had hoped to be in a new role already.

I reached out to one of my friends who worked there to update her about the date and time for the fourth interview. She said she was dying in suspense. I responded "I wish it as yesterday. I can't mentally or emotionally take much more with where I'm at right now. Every day I want to quit but I can't until I have another source of income."

My friend said, "You're almost there Rachel and this is how I know a breakthrough is on the way. Because right before it we are always at our breaking point. God is saying hold on just a little bit longer, you are literally days away from coming out on the other side."

I shared, "I had some serious ugly cries talking to God lately .. he knows how much I want this, but I also know that if I don't get the job it's literally because God said no, this is not where I want you and I have to fully trust that he has something better for me."

I absolutely loved her response, "I agree 100%. As much as we want something, to be outside of His will is such a scary place to be."

There was no doubt that I wanted what God had planned for my life far more than what I wanted based on my limited knowledge of what was to come. I wish I could say that I continued to hold firmly onto this belief.

When the day finally came for the interview, I had spent so much time praying and talking to God. I laid it all out on the table. I shared my hopes and my dreams. I shared my fears. I shared my concerns. I shared every thought that came into my head. I asked God to give me the words to answer their questions promptly, intelligently, and in such a way that demonstrated I was the right candidate for the job.

The interview was probably the most challenging interview I have ever had. It was clear they were looking for specific information. As I answered their questions, the vice president was constantly nodding in agreement, responding positively to my responses. The director was harder to read. There were times when I wasn't sure if he was even listening.

After about 30 minutes, the vice president started sharing what it was they were looking for. They were looking to change the culture to one where the employees felt valued and appreciated and less like a number.

As he was speaking, I couldn't help but smile. I had literally already sold myself without even knowing what it was they were looking for. I had shared about the ways I worked hard to improve employee moral at my former job. I spoke on all the ways I worked to create a positive work environment. I was literally everything they were looking for.

Despite not feeling as good about the director, I knew that the vice president was really impressed with me and he outranked the director so I felt quite confident that I would be offered one of the two positions. My interview was on Monday. They said they hoped to have a decision by that Friday.

On Wednesday, I received an email from the director around 6:30am asking when would be a good time to talk as he had additional questions for me. This made me nervous. I responded and let him know that I would be available any time. I didn't want to put it off.

When he finally called, he told me that he wanted to follow up on a question that had been asked to me during my third interview that had taken place with three of the supervisors and three of the agents who would be reporting to the new supervisor. Yes, there were six people in my third interview. He repeated the question and asked me if I remembered my answer. I did.

The question was something along the lines of tell me a time when you were faced with a difficult situation and how you handled it. He wanted me to give him my answer again as it was unclear from the notes made by the two who were supposed to be writing my answers.

This made me even more nervous as the response I gave involved a situation where a former direct employee had come to me once I was the department manager to express concerns of racism with her new supervisor. I explained, again, what happened and what steps I took following to ensure the matter was handled appropriately.

He wanted to know what additional steps had been taken. I explained that there were no additional steps taken as our entire site had been laid off, but I was thinking to myself *if I took additional steps, don't you think I would have included that in explaining what happened and what steps were taken to address it originally?*

He continued to make comments like, "so there was definitely something there but you don't know exactly what the issue was?" I went from being nervous to being annoyed. Part of me wanted to ask him *what would you have done?* Since my response didn't seen sufficient to him.

Mind you, I feel as though I did everything right. I would have liked to have done more but my hands were tied by a vice president who micro managed every aspect of our teams and would not allow us to even write an employee up without her approval. I could feel myself getting worked up. It really bothered me that he made it seem like I didn't do a good job addressing the issue despite explaining that the employee had come back to me after the fact and thanked me for continuing to push the issue and convincing her to move to a different team under another department manager. She didn't want to make waves with the supervisor, but I was a lot less concerned about the supervisor's feelings than I was with the well-being of the employee.

For the days following the call, I had a bad feeling in my gut about the director, his view of me, and my chances of getting the position.

Friday came and went and no word. It was hard but I waited until Wednesday before reaching out to the gentleman from human resources to see if a decision had been made. He informed me that they were still doing interviews and had not yet made a decision.

I knew that the third interview was supposed to take place on Thursday, so the fact that they were continuing to interview meant that they expanded beyond the initial three candidates. I was struggling. It was hard for me to stay positive. It was hard for me to stay in a place of gratitude. It was hard for me to keep the faith.

Another week went by and I decided to reach out to human resources again. The gentleman I had been working with usually responded within 30 minutes so when hours had passed, I took it as a sign. A bad one. I emailed around 10:30am. My phone rang at 4:30pm.

It was the gentleman from human resources informing me that I had not been selected for the position. It took everything in me to maintain my composure on the phone, to keep a positive and upbeat attitude until the minute I disconnected the call. Then I screamed.

Friends, I was so mad. I was beyond upset. I was straight angry.

God, how could you put me through all of this only to not get the job?

Five interviews. FIVE. And I wasn't chosen?

I was exactly what they wanted. It was who I inherently am, not someone I pretended to be to try to get a job.

I cried. I screamed. I wanted so badly to break something. Every ounce of me wanted to self-destruct. I considered buying half a gallon of ice cream and eating the whole thing. Or a bottle of wine and getting drunk. Or maybe I'd reach out to a guy I knew would drop everything and come over despite knowing I would be breaking almost a year of celibacy to focus on finding the man God wanted for me and not a man who filled the space.

I didn't know what to do, but I knew that I didn't want to wake up the next day not only sad but also in a state of regret.

I got in my car and drove 30 minutes to the cemetery. I needed to talk to my mom. I needed to go somewhere I felt safe to scream, to cry, to vent. I needed someone I could talk to about how angry at God I was.

I didn't deserve this. I'm a good person. I work so hard. I give 110% to a job that I hate for less than minimum wage. I deserve better.

When I got home from the cemetery, I went straight to bed and I cried some more. I didn't want to talk to anyone. I needed to be alone with all of the emotions I was feeling.

I always attend the Saturday night worship experience, but I didn't feel like going to church that Saturday. I didn't want to go praise and worship God. I didn't even want to talk to God right now. But I went regardless of how I felt.

It's amazing how God will meet you right where you're at. The sermon title was Make Room for the New. Pastor Steven said, "The hardest thing in the world is to just take it by faith. We talk a good game when it comes to faith. We say we're trusting in the Lord with all of our heart and not leaning into our own understanding. But it still creates a tension, which is how much should I trust God and how much should I try myself." He goes on to share how in the passage of scripture, the people are learning how to relate to God in a brand-new way.

I sat there with tears running down my face. This experience had certainly challenged me.

There were so many emotions. I didn't know how to process all of them. I had never been in a place like this emotionally before. I was so disappointed. I felt betrayed and abandoned by God. To go through so many interviews, to have everything on my side, and still not get the job.

It should have been easy for me to look at the situation and say, *okay this obviously isn't what God wants for me. He has something better in store*. But it wasn't. It wasn't easy for me to get over it at all.

I didn't want to talk to God. I was seriously acting like a child giving the silent treatment. Honestly, I'm embarrassed by the way I handled everything. It probably took me a month to normalize my emotions.

I tried very hard to refocus my energy on better things. I finished writing what I thought would be the last chapter of this book. I reached out to a couple friends and asked if they would read through it and give me their feedback. With something so deeply personal, I wanted to know how it would be received by those closest to me.

Once I had all the first drafts delivered, I needed something else to focus on. I had been browsing on Pinterest and came across this idea for hanging lights around your pool. I didn't want lights but I had always wanted plants. I sent it to my dad and asked him if he could help me.

The timing was perfect. My dad had been up north with his girlfriend. He flew home for a week so I thought I'd take advantage of the time he was in town. We went and bought 4x4's, quickset concrete and big planters. I thought if my dad could help me do one of them so I knew exactly what to do, I would be able to do the rest myself.

I kept saying I was only going to do a little at a time as I didn't want to spend a lot of money. Well, before I knew it, I had bought 5 planters and 10 plant hangers to put at the top of the 4x4's. Then I got the idea to paint my porch. I removed all the screen and cleaned the aluminum. As I was looking at it, I got the idea to run wires around the porch to have vines grow along to create a plant screen.

My dad's trip got extended and he ended up being in town for four weeks. He helped me fix my fence, remove two trees, do some concrete work, etc. I was on a mission to create a backyard oasis.

I was already $1200 into this project but I was so close to being done. All I needed was more potting soil and some small plants, so I decided to run to Walmart.

As I was walking out of Walmart, a former employee was walking in. I had no idea he was living in town again. He had moved away after we got laid off. We were both happy to see one another. We started chatting and he told me that he moved back to town because he was having a hard time finding a job in Jacksonville. That surprised me since it's a major city and where I live is not.

I asked him where he was working and when he told me I kind of made a cringing face. I had heard a lot of negative things about working there. He had heard the same and was apprehensive about applying but did anyway. We chatted for at least 30 minutes. As we started wrapping up, he asked me to send him my resume.

I'll be honest. I was apprehensive, but I sent it to him. He sent me a link for a job to apply for. It was entry level, but I wasn't exactly in a position to be picky.

The next day, which was a Friday, he forwards me an email from the hiring manager. Oddly enough, he had also worked with us before. He never worked for me but he remembered me. The email said, "Yes, I remember her. I liked her. Is she interested in my assistant manager position?" Assistant manager position?

My friend didn't know there was even an assistant manager position open. It wasn't listed on the job postings. My friend said he also sent my resume to his contact in human resources. He said I would probably hear something by Tuesday.

On Monday, I received a call from the hiring manager. He was definitely excited to talk to me. He told me that when he saw my resume, he was so excited he couldn't stop talking about me. His wife told him to calm down and he said he couldn't because I was exactly who he needed.

He shared with me that he had only been in the position for two months and the department was a bit of a mess but that's exactly why he needed someone like me. There was another assistant manager who was a systems expert. He needed a people expert.

I was flattered that what he remembers of me was how well I managed people. Quite frankly, I was flattered by the whole conversation. When I asked the start date, his response was "tomorrow?" I laughed and said that I would need to give a two-week notice to my current employer. He understood.

The next day I heard from a gentleman from human resources. He went through some of the specifics of the job, but we laughed a lot. He asked me if I could be available for an interview with the director on Friday. I was supposed to be out of town breaking down a unit that day but I could make sure to be in a quiet area. He commented how this (me being hired) seemed like a no brainer but I'd still have to talk to the director so he could sign off on it.

Not even an hour after my call with HR I received a call from the hiring manager. He wanted to know if I could talk to the director the next day instead. He really didn't want to delay it any longer than necessary. I laughed and said of course! I asked if there was anything I should know before going into it that would ensure it went well.

You know someone really wants to hire you when they tell you the exact 4 or 5 questions that the interviewer always asks. He shared with me that the director had career ambitions to be a Vice President and he wanted to be the director. I told him that worked out well since I planned on taking his position as manager. He loved it.

The next day, Wednesday, I spoke with the director for about an hour. I thought it went really well, but I find phone interviews really hard to gauge. I prefer to look someone in the eyes when I speak with them. He gave me some more specifics about the role but said that ultimately, it was the hiring manager who would make most of the decisions.

Knowing that the director had career ambitions himself, I was not shy about mine. In fact, I think he really liked how forward I was about it. He told me that he had shared with the hiring manager that he needed to hire someone who was going to push him. I smiled and laughed inside. He was talking to the right girl if he wanted someone who was going to push to do better and be better.

There had been a lot of conversation with the hiring manger, the gentleman from human resources and the director about salary. The hiring manager said his biggest concern is that they would not be able to pay me my asking price. Of course, he knew roughly what I was making at our previous job.

I couldn't exactly say "Oh don't worry about that, I'm not even making $30,000 a year right now." I wanted him to push for me to get as much money as they were willing to pay.

The gentleman from human resources told me that $54,000 was likely the highest they could go. I told the hiring manager and the director that I would really like between $55-$60,000. The worst that could happen was they told me no.

I kept hoping to receive a call on Wednesday with an offer. When I spoke to the gentleman from human resources on Tuesday, he said he would likely extend an offer the same day if the director gave the go ahead. I tried to keep myself busy by working on the yard.

Thursday morning, I ran to Lowes to grab something and of course, my phone rings. I see it's them. My heart starts to race.

I answered the phone excitedly and the gentleman from human resources was probably more excited than I was. He told me that they would like to offer me the job and were going to meet me in the middle of my asking salary. But it gets better. Not only would I get my salary, but I was also eligible for overtime.

I started laughing and said "I absolutely accept!" Mind you, I'm standing in the middle of an isle at Lowes on the phone with him laughing. He said that he would email me over the information for a background check and drug test.

Now, you know, I have been through some things financially in the last couple years so my credit score is not the best. I was really nervous about applying to work at a financial institution because of it. I specifically asked the gentleman from HR if there was anything else I needed to pass, clear or overcome in order to be hired. He assured me that it was only state and federal background and the drug test.

For so long, I had refrained from applying for jobs in my former field for fear that I would get hired only to have the job offer rescinded due to my credit score or bankruptcy. I was in complete shock, but I was standing in the middle of Lowes so I had to contain myself.

As soon as I got into my car, I started crying. I called my dad immediately to tell him that I got the job. He may have been more excited than I was. No one knows the struggles, the disappointments, and the heartache quite like my dad.

I immediately went and got the drug test done and completed the background information. Not long after I got a call from the hiring manager. He wanted to confirm the soonest I could start provided they got the background and drug test results. It felt good to be so wanted.

We chatted more about the job. He asked me how much I knew about different federal regulations. He offered to send me the book he used to pass the mortgage loan originator exam so I could read up before I started. It made me feel like he wanted to set me up for success from the moment I walked through the doors.

I was so excited. I couldn't believe how everything happened so fast. I called my brother to let him know first before calling my sister-in-law. I let her know that I would still finish the units that I'd booked on the east coast if the timing lined up and I could break the unit down and clean it on a weekend. She was in agreement so everything seemed fine.

I went through all of the units that I booked and created a document with all the necessary information to ensure that things continued to run smoothly after I was gone. There was even a part of me that felt guilty as silly as that sounds. As unhappy as I was, I didn't want to leave them in a position where they were negatively impacted.

I emailed all the information over to my sister-in-law and let her know that I would update the bonus sheet so everything was up to date with the vacate dates we had up to this point. I never received a response from my sister-in-law. She sends me a text later that day asking when my last day would be so that she could get organized. Nothing else was said about the information I had emailed over

The next day, I get an email from my brother full of fluff about how happy he was for me but this email was to inform me that my last paycheck would be on the 8th and it would include my pay and bonus through that date. He then went on to tell me that May would be the last month my cell phone bill would be covered. I could either open my own account or send him the money for my portion as they had not hit the lottery and he couldn't be a gravy train.

I sat there in shock. Complete disbelief of what I had just read. Even if it hadn't been from my brother and it was from my employer, I would have been offended. I worked so hard for them. I went above and beyond. I treated it as if it was my own company and now, I felt like I was being taken out with the trash.

I called my dad and read the email to him with tears running down my face. I felt bad turning to my dad about the pain his son had caused me but there's really no one else who would understand it either. I had called my dad crying many times in the weeks and months leading up to this. He knew every hurt feeling, every frustration, every struggle I was facing.

After I calmed down, I called my brother and asked if that was his way of telling me that he wasn't going to pay me the remaining bonuses I had for the units that I booked. He said he wasn't. That the bonus was for the work being done for those units while they were occupied. A bonus is for work and I wasn't working anymore.

I could feel my blood pressure going up. I knew my face was getting red from anger. I explained that the basis for the bonus was booking the unit and nothing else. There was no other stipulation attached to earning the bonus. It was built into what the client paid so it took no money out of their pocket. He just kept saying it was business to which I responded no, it was bull shit, but if that's how he wanted to do this. Again, he said it was business.

I was so mad. I was hurt. This is not how you treat your sister who had worked tirelessly for you. Who's 1099 for 2019 showed only $21,000 being made. You don't take money out of the pocket of the person who had put so much into yours. It was wrong. All of it.

I got my last pay check on the last day I was working for my sister-in-law. It was $1200 less than I expected it to be as she only paid me for 8 days' worth of my May bonus. The money I expected to have to go clothes shopping so I would have enough to get me through the first two weeks. I took a deep breath and reminded myself that God had brought me this far. This set back was not going to hinder anything that was to come. God's promises were alive in my life and that was what I chose to focus on.

I decided to take a week for myself before starting my new job. I wanted to finish up some projects I had started around the house. I needed the time to decompress from everything that happened with my brother. I wanted to go into this next chapter with nothing but excitement and gratitude.

As I started my new job, I was met with nothing but excitement and gratitude from my boss. He was probably more excited for me to be there than I was. It was such a great feeling. Within the first two weeks, I started writing down notes of things that I wanted to do, reports I wanted to have created, etc. I talked to my boss about it and his response was always, "that's a great idea, do it!"

I have been empowered from the moment I walked through the door to create the culture that I wanted to create, to manage the way I wanted to manage, etc. My boss, who is the manager, and his boss, who is the director, often ask me for my opinions on various things. They value my experience and point of view.

I am fortunate to have a boss who treats me as an equal and doesn't see his position as one of superiority. We have really good, open conversations that I believe has really helped us to identify where each of us can help the other. During conversation one day, I expressed that I had been concerned I may not get the position because of my credit score. I went on to tell him about being sued by my student loan company.

He shrugged it off and said that student loans and medical debts are looked at completely differently than other debts. In fact, his boss had been part of the admissions department at a college and he left because education had become a business. He hated what they were doing to young people who were trying to better themselves.

He then opened up and told me that he had filed bankruptcy back in 2010 after the market crashed. His background was in financial planning and people weren't investing like they had been. He explained how he had been offered a really great position but then they rescinded their offer when they saw he had a bankruptcy. He understood how sometimes things happen in our lives that are beyond our control.

Of course, I told him that I had filed bankruptcy too. I felt such relief in that moment as though I wasn't hiding anything. My boss knew exactly who I was and what I'd been through. It put me at such peace.

One morning I was driving into work and I started crying. I never imagined that things could work out this well. I felt like the quotes I had shared on social media in the past were coming to pass in my life. Even better than that I was seeing God's promises unfolding in ways that I never dreamed possible.

My life summarized in one verse -

> "Now to him who is able to do immeasurably more than all we ask or imagine, according to his power that is at work within us." Ephesians 3:20

As tears run down my face, friends, I want you to know that his word is true! His promises will come to pass. No matter how hard it gets, please don't ever stop believing that God is going to work all things out for your good.

Within the first three paychecks at my new job, I was able to get caught up on all of my bills. The check that I'll be receiving at the end of this week is pure savings. Can you believe that? I paid every single bill for the month out of my pay check this month. Not only do I not have any bills to pay out of this check, but I also have 40 hours of overtime. I will gross over $6000 this month. God brought me from an average of $2400 a month in a job I disliked, where I felt underpaid and underappreciated, to a place where I'm making more than that per pay check with a boss who speaks success over my life almost daily.

I am beyond thankful for the struggles that have made me into the person that I am today. I didn't always love it while I was going through it, but I know that it was necessary for God's will to come to pass in my life. I love the woman that God has turned me into through all of this.

I suppose I got my happily ever after ending after all. I know that you will to. Keep fighting friend. Keep pushing. Never give up on yourself. God is always with you. He goes before you, He stands beside you, and He always has your back. You are surrounded by God's faithfulness. I bet you'll start seeing it if you look for it like I did.

Be blessed.

ABOUT THE AUTHOR

While spending much of her life living for herself, Rachel Marie experienced a great deal of success. Graduating from law school in her mid-twenties, and becoming an Assistant Vice President of one of the biggest banks in the world in her early thirties. Yet, none of those accomplishments ever gave her a sense of wholeness.

It wasn't until everything came crashing down that she realized nothing she had ever accomplished was due to her own abilities. If it had been, she would have easily stepped into another upper management role with a new company. Instead, things got harder and harder. It was during this time a random stranger invited her to church and the trajectory of her life was forever changed.

Once a proud person who found her worth and value in worldly success, the last four years have taught her that the greatest gift we have as Christians is our testimony. Sharing what God has done in our lives allows us to help others find freedom.

For this reason, Rachel Marie decided to share her most intimate struggles, deepest feelings, and examples of God's never-ending faithfulness with the world.